What People are Saying about *The Rewired Life*

"As the founder of a movement whose mantra is "We are all recovering from something," I couldn't be more impressed with Erica's Spiegelman's most recent *Rewired* offering. Inspirational in its simplicity, straight-forward, strengths-based, and holistic—Erica's practical road-map is an exceptional starting point for all of us looking to be the next, best version of ourselves."
　　　—Dawn Nickel, PhD, founder of SHE RECOVERS

"Erica lays out the multi-faceted complexity of life in a simple way, showing that through a mix of emotional awareness, better self-care and daily habits, you have the power to feel the way you want in your life!"
　　　—Randy Spelling, motivational speaker and author of
　　　Unlimiting You: Step Out of Your Past and Into Your
　　　Purpose

"*The Rewired Life* is a practical guide that holds your hand as you work towards reprogramming and rewiring the parts of your life that are not operating at their optimal level. From self-love to our relationship with technology, exercise to living a balanced life, Erica Spiegelman touches on a myriad of topics by challenging the reader to look at their limiting beliefs and create an intentional plan to rewire their lives. With tips, tools, affirmations, and research-backed evidence, Spiegelman's step-by-step guidance and gentle approach helps the reader courageously lean into creating the life they're capable of living."
　　　—Vienna Pharaon, LMFT, founder of Mindful Marriage
　　　and Family Therapy and relationship expert for
　　　Motherly

"Erica's down-to-earth and practical approach helps inspire the masses to take action in their lives. *Rewired Life* integrates challenging concepts in an accessible way with built-in accountability for each aspect of your life. This book is honest, authentic and has something for everyone—wherever they perceive themselves to be in the journey to self-discovery and healing."

> —Bizzie Gold, founder of Break Method and personal development expert

"*The Rewired Life* could have the answers you have been looking for. Many people do not realize that our brains are being programmed from the minute we are created in our mother's womb. Throughout our life, we endure traumas that we don't even realize are trauma. We are wired by this fear and in constant survival mode. This book could be a way for you to start rewiring the patterns and habits that are keeping you stuck. This book helps you overcome the obstacles you are facing and have the life you deserve."

> —Ken Seeley, CCMI-M, CIP, CTP, author of *Face It and Fix It*

"Erica's new book *The Rewired Life* is full of wisdom that we all need for every area of our lives. From nutrition, to sleep, to self-care, she walks you through step-by-step how to rewire your brain to achieve its best in each vital area of your life. Erica's insight is relatable to all ages and stages of life and her simple yet expert outlook makes the tips and tools she suggests easy to implement to get the results you are looking for. I highly recommend this book for anyone who is looking for major breakthroughs or simply in need of time-tested knowledge to remind you to keep going and growing in life!"

> —Brittney Castro, CFP®, AAMS®, CRPC®, founder and CEO of Financially Wise Inc.

"In the world of personal development and making changes in the trajectory of our lives, there is no shortage of tips. Most are scattered on the beach like shells, as we struggle to make these tips part of who we are. It seems too hard and we remain unfulfilled, unable to become them. No longer just words of suggestion, Erica Spiegelman has found a way, through daily practice, to turn the most powerful of these into real and lasting shifts. Using clear explanations and profound yet simple affirmations, *The Rewired Life* creates the pathway to the best versions of who we have always wanted to be. This book can truly change your life."

—Bob Litwin, performance coach and author of *Live the Best Story of Your Life*

ERICA SPIEGELMAN

THE REWIRED LIFE

ERICA SPIEGELMAN

THE REWIRED LIFE

CREATING A BETTER LIFE THROUGH
SELF-CARE AND EMOTIONAL AWARENESS

hatherleigh

Improve your life. Change your world.

Improve your life. Change your world.

Hatherleigh Press is committed to preserving and protecting the natural resources of the earth. Environmentally responsible and sustainable practices are embraced within the company's mission statement.

Visit us at www.hatherleighpress.com and register online for free offers, discounts, special events, and more.

The Rewired Life
Text copyright © 2018 Erica Spiegelman

Library of Congress Cataloging-in-Publication Data is available upon request.
ISBN: 978-1-57826-780-4

Cover Design by Carolyn Kasper

Interior Design by Cynthia Dunne.

Printed in the United States
10 9 8 7 6 5 4 3 2 1

CONTENTS

Preface   xi

Introduction   xv

Chapter 1:   **OUR THOUGHTS**   1

Chapter 2:   **AUTHENTICITY**   15

Chapter 3:   **SELF-CARE**   29

Chapter 4:   **NUTRITION**   53

Chapter 5:   **EXERCISE**   77

Chapter 6:   **SLEEP**   91

Chapter 7:   **COMMUNICATION**   107

Chapter 8:   **TIME MANAGEMENT**   119

Chapter 9:   **VALUES**   133

Chapter 10:   **EVOLUTION**   147

Chapter 11:   **TECHNOLOGY**   159

Chapter 12:   **BALANCE**   173

Chapter 13:   **LOVE**   183

Chapter 14:   **COGNITIVE DISTORTIONS**   197

Chapter 15:   **OUR STRENGTH**   211

Appendix: Affirmations for Rewiring Your Life   222

              Acknowledgments   225

              About the Author   227

PREFACE

Our lives on this Earth are shaped by innumerable forces—the people we encounter, the way we perceive the world to be, and how we view our emotional state of being. Believe it or not, the experiences we endure shape our thoughts and affect how we relate to every area of our life.

The narratives and the self-talk that exists in our minds shape our decisions, our self-esteem, and how we interact in social situations, at work, and in our families. Most of us have absorbed both positive messaging and negative messaging along the way. When our caretakers, friends, teachers, and mentors showed us their pride, support, and love, it helped build our confidence and bolster our sense of self. But when the negative messages hit us, we took them to heart, as well, and may even now be mistakenly playing them over and over for years, even though they serve no worthwhile purpose in our lives.

I remember being in third grade, when my teacher told me that math was not my strong suit and that I should therefore focus my energies on what I *was* good at—English and history. More creative endeavors, in other words. For years, I would remember that day, that narrative that I would never be good at math, and decided to forget about learning any further. That conversation with my teacher rooted itself in my psyche. I stopped trying in math, to the point where on my SAT, I skipped any math questions that looked hard. I didn't even try.

Now, I run a business and know I am capable of learning *anything*, especially numbers. Things have changed; the narrative changed when I became aware of where that crazy thought had come from, the under-lying cause of why I thought what I did. I made the choice to learn, to take action and do my part to understand numbers. And I realized it's not that hard after all.

This is just an example of how one tiny moment in time can have a ripple effect on how a person's life unfolds.

We all have moments like this; moments that shaped and molded how we view ourselves. Here and now, make the decision not to let someone else's perception, view, or judgment about who you are define you, define your self-worth.

In my first book, *Rewired: A Bold and New Approach to Addiction and Recovery,* my intention was to help people change their lives for the better and teach a new way of living, free from substance abuse, destructive patterns, toxic relationships, and limiting self-beliefs. I wrote *Rewired* to share my journey and provide others with tools anyone can use to recover and find hope in their lives.

Then, something happened. Many people who were not dealing with addiction issues read my book; they left lovely reviews on Amazon, or reached out via email to tell me how *Rewired* has impacted their lives, all without having had addiction issues. They related to the subject matter that I discussed, such as open communication, healthy relationships, love, authenticity, and time management, even though the majority of the book was not directed towards them.

That's when I decided to create *The Rewired Life*, a book for everyone, whether you have had destructive habits or not. This book is for those who have the courage to ask the bigger questions in life, who want to understand how the chatter in their heads got there and how to change it. It's for everyone wanting to lead healthier lives mentally, physically, emotionally, and spiritually.

At the end of each chapter, I've included affirmations to help guide you on your first steps towards changing, understanding, and getting to know better your own personal narratives. Because once you understand how you're wired, you can get started rewiring your life to be happier and healthier.

Wishing you ALL the best,
—Erica

ERICA SPIEGELMAN

THE REWIRED LIFE

INTRODUCTION

"An influx of new research explores how our brains do continue to change and how our very thoughts impact those changes. This natural tendency of our brains to rewire is called neuroplasticity, which can be influenced by both external and internal factors."

—TINA HALLIS, SCIENTIST AND AUTHOR

The human brain has the incredible ability to reorganize its pathways by creating new connections between neurons. Referred to as neuroplasticity, this is the brain's startling secret—it never stops learning, changing, and adapting.

Deep-seated beliefs, damage, trauma, ruts, and bad habits can all be rewired. As far-fetched as it sounds, we can reprogram our brains in any way we choose. We have control over our thoughts, and by choosing to live a healthy, holistic lifestyle, we can literally rewrite our destiny.

It is never too early or too late to start rewiring our brains for optimal health. The common view—that we grow more set in our ways as we age—is a myth. The brain can form new strategies at virtually any age. We can overcome addictions, learn new languages, and come around to new points of view well into our senior years.

Just because you have been holding onto a certain way of thinking, living, or being for the bulk of your life doesn't mean you can't change the cards you've been dealt. But when we choose to tell ourselves the same stories for so long, over and over, we begin to accept that story as an established truth, rather than just one version of a much greater, constantly-evolving saga.

At any moment, you can take any card in your hand you dislike—your fear, shame, self-doubt, guilt, anger, distrust—and trade them in for a new hand. That is the beauty of neuroplasticity, and it is so awe-inspiring that it may take time for it to really sink in!

The only caveat is that rewiring must become a daily practice. It requires not only our participation, but our commitment—change won't happen passively. Rewiring is an active choice we must make for ourselves; in choosing to look at our lives and the paths that we have created, we are literally addressing the cognitive and emotional habits that hold us back.

We can ask ourselves daily, "What do I want to have happen in my life?" "How can I improve the quality of my relationships?" "How can I take care of myself better?" "How do I speak to myself, and what thoughts do I choose to entertain today?"

It's a daily check-in, examining our behaviors, patterns, and habits to see how they are serving us—or *not* serving us. It makes us better humans because it helps us be more present with ourselves.

There is tremendous accountability and responsibility in owning the power we have over our thoughts, speech, and daily habits. As we take ownership of our reality, moving towards greater authenticity, honesty, and courage, we are empowered beyond words. Instead of being helpless victims to our negative thinking, we become shining beacons for others who are suffering with the same lack of faith in themselves. We acquire a new purpose to our lives and seek new meaning.

With a practice of daily rewiring, our relationships improve, as does our physical, mental, emotional, and spiritual well-being. This book is meant to serve as a guide to help you explore each aspect of what it truly means to live a healthy life. Together, we will work on increasing emotional awareness, learn how best to nourish our bodies with adequate sleep, food, and exercise, improve communication skills, and identify the personal narratives we write everyday which stand in the way of our freedom and joy.

We will explore the ever-increasing role of technology in our lives, understanding how it both supports and complicates our attempts at self-care, and we will learn how to accomplish a sense of balance in all that we do.

It's important to have the gentle awareness that everything in our minds and bodies is working for our benefit; however, some coping mechanisms have become outdated, and that is why we are now addressing them. Making changes in our lives rests on the deep gratitude for the indomitable human spirit that can never be fully vanquished or kept down.

The following are short introductions to each of the chapters in this book, intended to help prepare you for its discussion, as well as help direct you to those areas you feel are most important in rewiring your life. This book can be read in any order, though we encourage you to read it cover to cover at least once—after all, each area of our life influences and is influenced by every other area, and a truly healthy life is one which achieves balance in all aspects. Each chapter will be followed by a set of affirmations on the topic that you can take away with you and apply to your daily life.

OUR THOUGHTS

Cultivating awareness of our own thinking process is difficult, since we are trying to evaluate something using the same mechanism that is itself under scrutiny. But it *is* possible to acquire a certain detachment, acknowledging the nature of our thoughts as something separate from our core worthiness and innate value, which always stays intact simply because we are human.

The truth is that our thoughts are responsive and vulnerable. If we grow up in a dysfunctional environment, our experiences may have molded our thinking in unfavorable ways. We may be prone to negative, self-defeating speech, a coping mechanism designed to protect us but which ultimately ends up damaging us further instead.

In this chapter, we will explore concrete tools for altering our thinking, setting things back on a positive, productive, and self-affirming path. We will cover how to choose a positive starting point for our day, changing our vocabulary, welcoming mistakes as part of personal growth, the cognitive distortions of globalizing and catastrophizing, the power of positive affirmations, and many other tools for creating a mental environment conducive to total well-being.

AUTHENTICITY

Many of us mistakenly believe that if we just conform well enough to what others expect from us—if we please them and fulfill their wishes—we will be loved and will receive the validation we so desperately need.

Unfortunately, the more we bend, twist, and obliterate our authentic self, the worse our relationships get. We grow to dislike ourselves, suppressing the talents, skills, and traits that are most innate within us. We may get sick physically, emotionally, and mentally, and be left wondering why.

Know that becoming more authentic can have a ripple effect on everyone in your life. Not everyone will be comfortable with your transformation, but we have to stay true to ourselves and know that, ultimately, we can be the most helpful to others when we are in alignment with our core values.

Removing our masks and dismantling our false selves takes time and a lot of work, but with just the slightest push in the direction of authenticity, you will be amazed and surprised as the difference you feel. You may uncover old cherished hobbies, old dreams and hopes, and sides of yourself you never knew existed, such as humor, empathy, or creativity.

In this chapter, we will discuss the stereotypical roles that are formed and maintained in a dysfunctional household, such as the Hero, the

Scapegoat, the Lost Child, the Mascot, and the Enabler. We will also talk about gender roles and what they mean to us, both in the past and in the present.

SELF-CARE

Emotional self-care must be part of our journey, as well. Self-care means embracing the idea of getting help from a professional counselor, clergy, or guide; it means exploring various forms of body work such as massage, reiki, and acupuncture; it means working on our communication skills and creating a sense of abiding trust in our relationships with others.

Self-care depends on a commitment to the spiritual nature of our souls. We can learn to cultivate healthy solitude, meditation, a connection with nature, and nourish a sense of gratitude and kindness towards all living things.

On top of that—although physical, mental, emotional, and spiritual self-care will probably keep you busy for a long time—there is yet more to cover: we must also care for ourselves socially and financially in today's complex, thriving world. Making time for fun, for dating, and for giving back to others is essential. We also have to surrender to the reality that finances don't run themselves. Learning to use a budget, keep accurate records, asking for raises and promotions, and even starting our own business (if we feel so inclined) are elements of modern self-care.

In this chapter, we will delve into what it means to practice daily self-care in all areas of our lives. We will examine physical self-care, including our diets, our exercise routines, how well we sleep, and how well we physically present ourselves to the world. Addressing mental self-care, we will talk about managing our time, dealing with stress, being assertive in the world, and achieving balance in our everyday activities.

In short, this chapter will cover every possible facet of what it means to love yourself and act upon that love daily.

NUTRITION

The effects of good nutrition and a healthy diet cannot be underestimated. What we put in our bodies on a daily basis shapes our perception, our feelings, our energy levels, and our whole outlook on the day.

There is untold literature available about what to eat and how to eat it, but what we really need to tackle is our underlying resistance to properly caring for our physical bodies. We may be carrying unconscious messages within us about our eating or our weight, often tied to early experiences of trauma and abuse. Food becomes a battleground upon which our internal struggles are played out.

In this chapter, we will discuss the best ways of selecting, preparing, and cooking different foods, as well as the underlying structure of food (as protein, fat, or carbohydrate). We will explore the need to drink enough water, and a few plans for eating that focus on balance and moderation. But beyond that, we will explore the personal narratives that are so integral to the practice of nutrition.

EXERCISE

Exercise is as important as brushing our teeth, yet many of us avoid it for a variety of reasons. In this chapter, we will explore our personal blocks against sports and physical activity, delving into such topics as childhood bullying, domestic violence, and dealing with obesity. We will ask important questions about how much exercise we all need and what types of exercise are best for us. From aerobics, strength training, and flexibility and balance exercises, there is so much to choose from, meaning each person can (and should) find their own unique relationship with exercise that works for their personality, interests, and lifestyle. There is no such thing as a one-size-fits-all exercise plan, and authenticity is as relevant in fitness as in any other area of your life.

SLEEP

Sleep is as important as breathing to our ability to function. Yet through a thousand forms of avoidance, we manage to rob ourselves of this vital element of life, resorting to stimulants to try to stretch the fabric of time to better accommodate our need for greater and greater productivity and achievement.

In this chapter, we will talk about how much rest each of us really needs and the different types of sleep we go through each night. We will explore the wide range of sleep disorders, from common insomnia to circadian sleep-wake disorders, parasomnia, night terrors, bruxism, and sleep drunkenness.

This chapter will also offer gentle ways to improve our sleep with herbs, visualization, and meditation. We will look beneath the obvious to discover why it may be frightening to surrender to sleep, and what drives each person to run from the single most nourishing act in their day.

COMMUNICATION

As humans, we have achieved the incredible ability to use language to express our thoughts and feelings. Yet it is astonishing how hard it can be for some of us to connect with others, be direct, and own our desires, preferences, and opinions.

Learning to practice healthy communication is a skill, one which you need to succeed in any profession and to sustain any type of lasting, intimate relationship, whether with family, friends, a lover, or even with acquaintances.

We may have experienced early trauma or abuse that twisted our communication patterns, causing us to become passive-aggressive, shut down, or even become violent. As adults, these failed communication strategies are preventing us from reaching our goals and we need to dismantle them before we can rebuild on solid ground.

In this chapter, we will explore what it means to actively listen to others, to hold space for them and to not take things personally. We'll talk about what it means to function in a world with high-speed technology at our fingertips, and how this can both help and hinder our efforts to reach out. Finally, we will discuss body language and other forms of non-verbal communication and delve into the joys—and terrors—of public speaking.

TIME MANAGEMENT

Today we can travel to outer space, perform complex brain surgery using virtual reality software, and communicate via social media with people in every corner of the world. But despite our mind-blowing advances in technology, we are still subject to the immutable laws of time. No matter what we do, we cannot make more, or fewer, hours in the day. We must abide by the same time constraints as our ancestors and find ways to effectively manage the time that we are given.

In this chapter, we will learn how to track our time to discover exactly how, where, and why we are wasting it. We will work on blocking out harmful distractions, setting time limits for tasks, and dealing with the specter of workaholism and its ill effects. Finally, our perfectionism, our cultural addiction to caffeine, and our ability to prioritize and delegate tasks will all come under scrutiny.

VALUES

To live the most authentic life possible, we must define and declare our core values: those innate beliefs and assumptions that drive us, inform our actions, and inspire both ourselves and others. Yet there are a million situations in which we are tempted to compromise our value systems, and we must uncover these in order to heal and move forward.

When we encounter no-win scenarios, especially in childhood, we are tempted to defer our values to survive in a toxic or abusive situation. At those times, we may choose to placate an angry authority figure rather than speak our minds; or, we may have chosen to just pay the bills for our families, rather than pursue a calling that speaks to our hearts but which isn't as financially stable.

In this chapter, we will explore the core values of highly successful and spiritual people, including integrity, passion, excellence, responsibility, commitment, confidence, perseverance, compassion, patience, and, last but not least, gratitude.

EVOLUTION

The Earth, with all its animals, flora and fauna, is in a constant state of evolution. Everything around us is changing, growing, developing, and moving forward, yet we sometimes get stuck in a rut and just refuse to change. We find ourselves stagnating, unable to grow up, clinging to outmoded ways of operating, thinking, and relating with others.

In this chapter, we will root out the reasons why we may self-sabotage and find a path towards being our most productive and capable selves. We will talk about how important it is to surround ourselves with those who inspire us and serve as positive role models. We will learn to face our fear of being hurt again, our fear of not measuring up, and our fear of the unknown. We will boldly move past our fears, both of failure and of success.

TECHNOLOGY

Ethically navigating today's exponentially evolving technological land-scape is one of the greatest challenges we face as human beings in the twenty-first century. We must constantly weigh our personal ethics against the increasing possibilities that are available to us almost daily. We must figure out a way to make technology serve our highest good, rather than become slaves to it.

In this chapter we will discuss how technology has affected our personal relationships, from dating online to choosing texting, social media, and apps over face-to-face connection.

We will also explore the ways in which we hide behind the digital versions of ourselves and the evolution of the "cyber-bully," as well as examine what privacy means in the digital age, and how the concepts of freedom of speech and language itself have been radically altered.

BALANCE

Various cultures, religions, and spiritual practices all seek to provide an answer to the question, "What is balance?"

Balance means learning to give and receive in equal measure. Many healing practitioners believe that imbalance is the root of suffering and disease, and that all things are connected. We cannot be spiritually sick and not see effects in our bodies and minds. Conversely, if we are physically ill, we will feel it mentally and emotionally, as well.

In this chapter, we will try to answer the question of what balance means to us. We will learn how to spend our time in a harmonious fashion, one that doesn't leave out any important aspect of being human. We need to make time for sleep, work, play, love, hobbies, travel, nature, and connecting with our deepest selves on a daily basis. What "balance" means to us will change from one day to the next, yet we can always strive to stay attuned to our inner voice that will tell us when we are shifting out of sync.

LOVE

Phrases such as "love makes the world go 'round" echo in our heads, even as we privately doubt whether this is truly the case. Love is that ubiquitous human energy that connects us with every other living thing, drives our passions, and which even has the ability to create new life.

When we're cut off from love, whether through a personal choice stemming from trauma and abuse, from a devastating personal loss, or from a past filled with neglect and emotional coldness, we suffer immeasurably. We simply cannot live without love in our lives, hard as we may try. We can substitute cookies, alcohol, sex, success, money, or possessions for love, but that won't be sustainable for very long. Eventually, we will face a spiritual crisis that will crack us open, and we will have to face our own humanity.

In this chapter, we will investigate the nature of love: what it is and what it *isn't*. We'll talk about selflessness, respect, trust, commitment, acceptance, forgiveness, empathy, patience, peacefulness, and honesty, and explore how these aspects allow us to experience deep intimacy and partnership with other human beings.

COGNITIVE DISTORTIONS

Cognitive distortions are mental filters that keep us from living in reality. These are the convincing mental tricks our minds play on us to keep us miserable, in fear, and in self-doubt.

Among these are catastrophizing, minimizing, caving in to "should's," polarized black-and-white thinking, overgeneralization, taking things personally, control fallacies, fairness fallacies, change fallacies, using emotional reasoning, mind-reading, and having to always be right.

In this chapter, we will explore the early roots of these distortions. How did they begin? How did they once support us? How are they now causing damage in our lives? How can we counter them by forming new habits and new neural pathways, rewiring our thinking for a more positive mental environment?

OUR STRENGTH

Gathering all the aspects of the previous chapters, we will explore how all forms of self-care and self-love work together to create a personal inner strength that is immutable and undeniable. We begin to look at our failures and struggles as lessons, knowing that everything in the Universe is conspiring for our good if we are willing to be active partners in our growth.

We can make the deep decision to reframe the negatives—whether it's a breakup, the death of a loved one, or the loss of a job—as something we can learn from. Strength comes from flexibility and flow, rather than from rigidity. Instead of power over others or our circumstances, we can cultivate the inner strength that comes from a daily commitment to living a healthy, loving life.

In other words, we must learn to seek strength by looking inwards, rather than grabbing at external fixes, which are ultimately fleeting. In this chapter, we celebrate our progress, our willingness, our openness, and our imagination, and give ourselves the credit we deserve for making it this far. We open up fully to the next chapter in our lives.

Chapter 1

OUR THOUGHTS

"One can have no smaller or greater mastery than mastery of oneself."

LEONARDO DA VINCI

Although we cannot see them, our thoughts are very real and are responsible for nearly everything that we manifest in our lives. Every building you see began as a design in the mind of the architect. So, too, with our lives: everything we experience is a result of our mental blueprints. Depending on the content of our thoughts, we can either build a palace or a slum. We can build peace, security, love, and kindness…or we can build chaos, betrayal, and fear.

Learning to take charge of our thinking, to take responsibility for the quality of our "thought life," is an integral part of the journey towards self-love and self-respect. You may think you have no control over your thoughts; you may even feel victimized by negative thinking that seems to never stop. But this is an illusion. Mastering one's mind is entirely possible, and by mastering your mind, you master your life.

Many of us have experienced some kind of trauma or damage in our lives that makes it difficult to think positively. We may have received messages early on that are hard to shake, such as the idea that we are somehow unlovable, unworthy, or untalented. We may have experienced physical, sexual, or verbal abuse that only reinforced our perceived worthlessness.

Learning to break the chains of these negative narratives is the work that lies before you if you want to achieve personal happiness, a sense of purpose, and a renewed sense of passion. It is challenging, but not impossible. This chapter will give you the tools you need to establish the sort of healthy mental atmosphere that translates to a healthy outer life, one full of abundance, rich relationships, career success, and giving back.

Many self-help gurus will simply tell you to "think positive" or to go meditate without realizing that these vague instructions leave many stranded, in need of a more structured approach to changing their negative thinking patterns. In the following pages, we discuss new, important strategies that you can use in addition to meditation to help begin restructuring your mental patterns for more joy, positivity, and inner peace.

CHOOSE A POSITIVE STARTING POINT FOR YOUR DAY

It is during those first few moments of consciousness each day, right after we wake up, that we enter the mental space we will occupy for much of the next twenty-four hours. If the first thing we do is to reach for our phones to browse Facebook, read depressing headlines, check your online dating accounts, or field texts from a distressed family member, we are cheating ourselves of the mental fuel we need to face the day.

Instead, I offer you the simple suggestion to begin your day by consuming positive, uplifting literature of some kind, or by taking a moment of positive meditation to reflect on gratitude and loving kindness. Perhaps these first five minutes can be spent connecting with your pets or enjoying the sunrise. There are many variations; the point is to make a choice—a choice to begin your day in a positive mindset.

Making a conscious effort to spend the first five minutes of your morning cultivating positive thoughts will make a huge difference throughout the day. As you do this each morning, you will begin to rewire the part of your brain that braces for catastrophe and doom each time your alarm clock rings. You will come to fondly anticipate opening your eyes each day.

To start, when you wake up, simply refuse to allow any distraction to interrupt your five minutes of positive self-reflection. This small, attainable change will reap huge benefits. Try it for thirty days and see if you experience a ripple effect.

CHANGE YOUR VOCABULARY

The brain, as we now know, is incredibly adaptable and is highly sensitive to the words that we use every day. How you describe and frame your experiences creates the thoughts and feelings these experiences inspire. Paying careful attention to the words you use is not only an exercise in mindfulness, but will actually alter your day-to-day experience.

A perfect example of this is the common experience of asking someone how their day is going. When someone used to ask me how I was, I would say, "I have to go to work," or "I have to exercise." Instead, I've learned to use the word "*get*." Changing these words— "have to" to "get to"—exemplifies for ourselves the great privilege we have. We "get to" go to school, we "get to" see our parents for Sunday night dinner. We are blessed with these opportunities, which many in this world do not have.

I noticed that several people around me were responding very enthusiastically to these types of answers, and it even began to resonate with others. So, go ahead—try to see your experiences in this positive manner as an honor or privilege.

As another example, my father-in- law, Izydor, when asked how he is, always replies with a resounding, "*Fantastic!*" It fascinated me very much, at first; he truly radiated energy, so much so that you truly believe he felt that way. So I decided to try answering in a positive manner on days when I was feeling all over the place or just sort of "blah" by saying I was "*Wonderful!*" when someone asked me how I was feeling. Lo and behold, my feelings did change. I felt more lighthearted, and I knew I was uplifting others instead of bringing them down.

This isn't to say that we can brush away real depression with mere words, but our words do matter a great deal, and they continuously shape our reality. So just for today, go ahead and describe your experience in positive terms. If you're nervous about driving, say, "I *am a fantastic driver!*" and know that it is true. If you feel a little frumpy, tell people, "I *am a fabulous, sexy human being!*" If you feel bored or thwarted at work, say, "*My job is easy and fun!*"

It can actually be a lot of fun to change your vocabulary!

WELCOME MISTAKES AS OPPORTUNITIES FOR GROWTH

Everyone makes mistakes. It's the most human attribute we have—our imperfection. It's what makes the human race so vulnerable and endearing; otherwise, we would be a race of robots, without opportunity for growth and self-expression. Learning to embrace our mistakes is learning to embrace our humanity. Once we can accept ourselves as we are, we can begin to extend this compassion and understanding outwards and find that others melt when they encounter our forgiveness and approval.

Successful people do not view mistakes as reflections of their worth. They don't take mistakes to heart. Rather, they value their mistakes as markers that can help guide them to success. In fact, they *welcome* mistakes as messengers of change and improvement.

Whatever your field or vision for your life, a mistake can help to set you on a more fitting path. If you've made a mistake in a relationship, think to yourself, "Thank you, mistake, for showing me what not to do next time." If you've made a mistake at work, own it and ask your boss how you can improve. Your employer will be so impressed by your humility, openness, and willingness, you may find the outcome to be the exact opposite of what you expected.

When our thoughts are clouded by shame, remorse, guilt, and frustration over our perceived mistakes, we create for ourselves a very heavy, uncomfortable mental environment. It's up to us to learn to shake off our mistakes quickly while still learning from them.

Above all else, remember that *you* are never a mistake; only your behavior is. We are always working with the information we have at that moment, doing our best with what we have available, so no one "should have" known better. We only know what we know at the time.

And now we know that mistakes are our friends.

RECOGNIZE YOUR "GLOBALIZING"

If you Google the term "globalization," you may find references to economic policies and corporate expansion. But there is another kind of globalizing that happens in our thinking when we take one instance and interpret it to apply to our *whole lives.*

If a truck happens to drive by and splatters mud all over you, you might think to yourself, "I always get screwed." This is an example of using one incident to create a global statement about yourself and your life, in error. A healthier mindset would be to think, "This is unpleasant, but it's not personal. Shit happens."

Some other common examples of globalized thinking include:
"Nothing matters."
"I suck."
"No one likes me."
"I'm a failure."
"This always happens to me."
Any time you hear those key words—"always," "never," "nothing," "everything"—you know you're in the trouble zone.

Take a moment when you hear these key words to consider whether you might be generalizing. It might be true that a particular individual doesn't like you; that's a common human experience, and it can't always be helped. But to extrapolate from that scenario the idea that *no* human beings like you, or that you are unlikeable, is a truly damaging train of thought, one that we can stop in its track through awareness.

We can fight back against the insinuations that our brain insists upon, stating flatly that we don't have enough information to make a statement like, "No one likes me." You can counter with, "No one? That's eight *billion* people. Seems inaccurate to me."

By constantly staying vigilant over our assumptions and our generalizations, we can live more in reality, accepting the grey areas. Black and white thinking is a real trap because it robs us of our joy and all the nuances and subtleties life has to offer.

RECOGNIZE YOUR "CATASTROPHIZING"

Catastrophizing refers to the bad habit many of us have of turning a bad situation into the *worst* situation. When something negative occurs, we use it to create a doomsday scenario about our whole lives, making up a story about our future, and succumbing to fear, worry, and doubt.

There many types of catastrophizing, but the most common is "future-tripping," where we think of all the things that might go wrong in a situation or relationship. This can be an alluring path to go down because it offers us the illusion of control. If we know the future ahead of time—even if that "future" is just a negative fantasy—then we have some measure of control over our life, and this is comforting.

Sadly, catastrophizing tends to produce a negative, self-fulfilling prophesy. We end up manifesting many of our deepest fears precisely because we have focused on them, visualized them, and fully bought into them. An example of this might be that, after having a fight with your significant other, you falsely believe that it will be "the end" and start acting accordingly.

In reality, a fight is not a catastrophe, but a normal event in even the most intimate relationships. Learning how to deal with setbacks requires patience and commitment to changing our thought patterns, but it *can* be done. We have to admit that we don't know the future and anything is possible. Saying simple, positive messages to ourselves can go a long way in reversing our tendency to catastrophize.

Some of these positive messages might include:

"Life is always changing. I might be down now, but things will change soon enough."

"Everybody makes mistakes. I'll do what I can to fix this, and I'll try to do better next time."

"I have what it takes to handle any situation that comes my way."

"If I don't have the solution, I can ask someone for help. I have what it takes to ask for help."

These types of positive reinforcements start to rewire our brains for more stability and realism in our lives. Try it out, and you'll start to see how every situation has several sides to it and how you can interpret adversity more as a challenge or adventure and less as a catastrophe.

USE POSITIVE AFFIRMATIONS

If you have had any exposure to the self-help community, or to therapy in general, you are probably familiar with positive affirmations. Affirmations are so helpful and so effective that there is a huge market for these types of books and audiobooks; in fact, several authors have made their fortune solely on coming up with catchy affirmations.

Affirmations are any positive statements that affirm something you would like to be true about yourself or your life. Some examples are:

"I am in the right place, doing the right thing at the right time."

"I have enough, I do enough, I am enough."

"I give and receive love with ease."

Why are affirmations so effective? Because, as we've learned, our thoughts *become* our reality. What we say to ourselves and affirm each day becomes our living, breathing experience. Everything in our world began as a thought. Your dining room table began as a thought in the furniture designer's mind before it became a blueprint and before it eventually landed on the showroom floor. Life is the creative process of putting our dreams and desires into words first, and then allowing them to manifest organically.

If you are someone who received a lot of negative messages as a child, then rewiring your brain for positive thinking will be somewhat of a challenge. But it can be done. It may require a commitment to a daily reversal of those old, worn-out tapes through a continuous and devoted recitation of your new reality.

"I am worthy." "I am valuable." "My thoughts and feelings matter deeply." As you hear these new messages, your brain will begin to respond. Your whole mental environment will start to flourish. But it doesn't happen overnight. It takes repetition to really break in a new groove in your brain.

You can use affirmations that are already written, or you can write your own. Many people like to listen to affirmations rather than read them. Another excellent trick is to say the affirmations to yourself in the mirror. "I am beautiful. "I am successful." "I am whole." I know others who write their affirmations on post-it notes and stick them all over the house. However you do it, whatever works best, is the right way for you.

LIST PROS AND CONS

This is a great exercise that tends to produce a lot of mental clarity. I know many clients who struggle with their decision-making process, getting bogged down by confusion and distress over choosing the right direction.

Know that at any moment, you can make a list of pros and cons for a decision. Once you do this, putting everything down on paper, you will be able to see more clearly what you really feel and think about a particular situation.

For instance, you may want to quit eating sugar. That is a great goal, as there are many drawbacks to eating sugar, including weight gain, lowered energy, and increased risk of diabetes. However, you might find that it is next to impossible to change your diet. When you write down the list of pros and cons for eating sugar, you might see that the pros include things like: sugar comforts you; it makes you feel closer to your family and your childhood; it's fast and convenient.

In fact, the list of pros may nicely balance the list of cons. It can lead to a lot of self-compassion and acceptance about a particular behavior when we can see clearly that we have good reasons for our inner conflict. This self-compassion can help soften our frustration over a decision and produce a more peaceful, pleasant mental environment. Our behavior is no longer a mystery to us, and the conflict may resolve itself without any struggle on our part.

A pros and cons list may also produce an instant acknowledgement of our real feelings about someone or something. If we have a list of reasons not to date someone that far outnumber our reasons for being with that person, then we've no choice but to face a truth that is hard to ignore.

KEEP A THOUGHT JOURNAL

On that note, there is something very powerful about putting our thoughts down on paper. It helps us to see patterns that we might be unaware of otherwise. Keeping a thought journal means taking the time each day to write down your most repetitive negative thoughts. Just get them down on the page; don't judge them, just collect them. Once you have about a week's worth, then you can examine them to see if a pattern emerges.

Looking at your thoughts: are they all related to fear and anxiety? Or are they mostly about guilt and shame? Perhaps they are all directed at a particular person, manifesting as an intense obsession or infatuation. These distinctions are important if you want to work on positive thinking.

By figuring out your normal patterns of negativity, you can rewrite your thought grooves using strategic, well-chosen affirmations that contradict the self-sabotaging mechanisms. You may also realize that you are dealing with an addiction of some kind, whether it be to food, sex, money, or drugs and alcohol, which you can seek help for. Writing down your thoughts is another way of taking control of your mental space. It's about taking back your power.

RECOGNIZE THE PESSIMISTS, NAYSAYERS, AND NEGATIVE NELLIES IN YOUR LIFE

If you want to change your thinking, you may have to begin by being more particular about the company you keep. Thought patterns can be highly contagious; when we surround ourselves with people who espouse negative, limiting beliefs, it can be quite difficult to hold our own fragile blossoming mindset intact. Hearing others constantly say, "You can't," "You won't," "You shouldn't," and "You will never," is like absorbing poison.

We cannot afford to take these types of life views to heart. Take note of who in your life tends to bring you down and think twice about sharing your progress with them. If someone always rains on your parade, you may have to be more protective of your mental environment. Spend more time with people who support your dreams. Make a list of people who are on your team in life. Gather your supporters close and keep the negative Nellies at arm's length.

One of the biggest sources of negativity in modern life is the media. We all want to remain well-informed on current events, but the "news" is often mental pollution, casting a shadow of chaos and disaster on our day. There is a reason why most of the news is bad news—negative thinking is addictive. It's not healthy to constantly focus on all that is going wrong with the world. We know it's out there, but we have a choice regarding what we consume, media-wise.

Take time to seek out the "good" news in the world. Find others who are doing good deeds, people who are making the world a better place, and celebrate them. Getting hooked on the depressing carousel of tragedy in the nightly news is a mental trap we can avoid with a little discernment and research.

MAINTAIN A HEALTHY BODY

It may seem counterintuitive, but without a healthy body, there can be no healthy mind. Our thoughts are so often a product of our physical state. When we are tired, hungry, depleted, malnourished, or starved for physical touch, our negative thoughts become alarms, letting us know we are out of balance.

Learning to nurture ourselves physically is all-important for establishing a pleasant, calm mental environment. Eating right and exercising are mandatory if we want to overcome negative thinking. I have never met a single person who didn't feel uplifted mentally after going for a thirty-minute jog.

Sleep is also imperative. We need enough rest to repair our minds, to process our day, and to relax our muscles. If we are short on sleep, we need to learn to forgo our tendency to take our negative thoughts seriously. Instead, we can say to ourselves, "I'm tired. This will look different tomorrow."

Finally, an adult can no more live without physical touch than a baby can. When we have not been touched in a long time, our thoughts can turn on us, becoming paranoid, anxious, or biting. If we are not in a relationship, we can learn to receive therapeutic touch from a massage therapist, or even learn to receive warmth from a hot tub or sauna. This is important, as when we feel held and physically supported, our thoughts tend to grow more positive and hopeful.

RELEASING RAGE

While a healthy release of anger and rage falls under the category of maintaining a healthy body, it deserves its own section since it is a unique topic.

Rage is a natural response to abusive situations, yet if you were abused as a child, you may never have had the chance to release this rage, as you probably weren't able to process it at the time. Also, as children our survival depends on our caretakers, so it's rare that we choose to threaten our survival by expressing rage at the person who is feeding us or taking care of us.

Therefore, many of us arrive in adulthood with a surplus of suppressed or repressed rage, which creates a host of problems for us both mentally and physically. We may find that we suffer from depression, repetitive, obsessive thinking, and irrational fears. Rage acts as a type of pressure, pressing down on our minds, compressing our thoughts so that they are narrow, painful, and cramped.

To combat this problem, we need to devote time to a healthy release of residual rage in private, so that it does not negatively affect anyone around us. We can do this in our car, in a private space, or in a safe support group. Even just screaming and hitting a pillow can help ease the mental buildup of unhealthy anger that is sabotaging our lives. As we let the rage out, we start to feel calmer, more centered, happier. There is suddenly more room in our minds for positive thoughts, for hope, and for spontaneity.

There should be no fear that anger is never-ending. Remember that abuse was finite; we survived it, and we are now in the phase of getting healthier. Just reading this book is a sign of that. Never fear that the anger will consume you. You will simply get it out of your system, and that will be the end of it.

A WORD ABOUT MEDICATION

In today's landscape of instant gratification, many doctors prescribe antidepressants and other pharmaceuticals rather quickly, and these aids can be very helpful to those that truly need them. There are cases where therapy and mental tools like affirmations are simply not enough to combat negative thinking, especially when OCD, dysthymia, or chronic anxiety are to blame.

Medication can help you to establish a more favorable chemical environment while you work on practicing your everyday tools for positive thinking. A combination of medication and therapy is often the best solution for those who find themselves stuck in a mental rut.

I hope you have gathered from this chapter that there is a plethora of concrete tools you can use to help reverse your negative thinking habits and start living in harmony with your mind. No one should have to suffer from painful, repetitive thoughts, or be alone within a mind that has turned on itself. The mind is a prison that no one belongs in.

As we establish new, healthy patterns of thinking about ourselves and our lives, our brains begin to rewire naturally for success and freedom. Eventually our minds become vehicles of self-support, and the new patterns operate on their own without effort. Once we have put in the work, the work takes over and our minds begin to run on a new, healthy auto-pilot in a positive direction—going forward.

Taking the Next Step

On the next page are twenty affirmations to help rewire your thoughts. You can use these as you see fit; perhaps writing them down and posting them in your personal space or recording them for playback at a later time. Just by reading them right now, know that you are opening yourself up to new possibilities—and that is all it takes to initiate change.

Affirmations for Our Thoughts

- I choose to think the best about myself and other people.
- Today, I choose to focus on what is working in my life.
- I believe in myself unconditionally.
- Everything is unfolding in perfect timing.
- Everything I say, do, and feel makes a difference.
- I am loved, supported, and protected.
- I am in the right place, doing the right thing at the right time.
- I have enough, I do enough, I am enough.
- I give and receive love with ease.
- Negative thoughts no longer hold any power over me.
- Today, I begin to utilize my abundant gifts and talents.
- I have everything I need to be successful in my life.
- I base my happiness on my blessings.
- I release myself from the need to compare to anyone else.
- Everything is happening for my ultimate good.
- I treat my body with respect and adhere to its limits.
- I find healthy outlets for my anger and frustration.
- I find it easy to ask for help when I need it.
- I have what it takes to be happy and productive.
- Every day is a new chance to rewrite my life.

AUTHENTICITY

"The privilege of a lifetime is to become who you truly are."

—C.G. JUNG

Why do we find children so delightful? There are any number of reasons, but one in particular is because they lack the guile to be anything but completely genuine in their speech, actions, and emotions. They speak from the heart, and this can surprise us and make us laugh because as adults, we have learned to mask and repress much of our authenticity.

Being authentic means returning to that childlike state of complete honesty, when we had nothing to hide and nothing to be ashamed of. It means becoming the author of our own lives and not letting any person, place, or thing influence us to shut down or turn our back on our own values and opinions. It means making decisions based on our finely-honed intuition and our deeply rooted connection with ourselves and the Universe, rather than out of fear that others won't like us or will abandon us.

The price for not living an authentic life can be very high indeed. It can result in physical illness, aches and pains, depression, boredom, and anxiety. It can take a heavy toll on the quality of our relationships, which inevitably lack intimacy when we're pretending to be someone else. It can keep us from finding fulfilling, joyful work, and thus from prospering and living a life of financial abundance. It can thin the fabric of our peace of mind and interrupt our spiritual growth.

Learning to understand and dismantle our defense mechanisms so that we can begin living authentically—either once more or, in some cases, for the first time—takes dedication, patience, and supreme compassion for oneself. It isn't easy, especially in a competitive, materialistic Western culture where we're always subtly influenced by advertising to have more, be more, and do more. Living in an environment of 24/7 social media doesn't help matters either, as we're constantly in danger of comparing ourselves to others.

But it *can* be achieved, and when you're finally living in a state of authenticity, the benefits are immeasurable. You will feel as though the whole world is an open, magical adventure to explore, and you will start to make the sorts of positive contribution to this planet that only you are capable of.

This reminds me of an amazing quote by the modern dance genius Martha Graham, which states, "There is a vitality, a life force, an energy, a quickening that is translated through you into action, and because there is only one of you in all time, this expression is unique. And if you block it, it will never exist through any other medium and will be lost."

If you are serious about learning to live in authenticity, it might be a good idea to print this quote and hang it where you can read it and see it every day. Remember just how special you are and how much you have to offer the world.

FACING EARLY CONDITIONING

So what goes wrong? Where did we lose that childlike authenticity and start covering up our true feelings, thoughts, and opinions?

The truth is that this can happen at any point during our lives. We may have grown up in an atmosphere of invalidation and had our true selves laughed at, rejected, and shamed. In those cases, it's no wonder we dove inwards and made a promise never to show our cards again. We may have grown up in an environment filled with rage and screaming and determined that it was always better not to rock the boat and not risk angering a caregiver or guardian. Or we may have experienced neglect at home, with no one to ask us how we felt or what we thought, to the point where we are strangers to ourselves and we don't really know what is authentic for us.

It can be a very empowering and eye-opening experience to sit down and start writing about our early experiences, helping us to pinpoint exactly where we made the inward decision to stop being ourselves and start being what we thought "they" wanted us to be.

See if you can spend twenty minutes writing down any early memories you have of losing your authentic voice. Was there a time when you told your parents you wanted to be a singer and they told you it wasn't practical? Was there a moment when you wanted to kiss someone of the same sex and you were told that "God" didn't approve of such behavior? Were you told that you were too "emotional" because you cried easily? Were you told that girls shouldn't play football or run through the house?

There are a million tiny moments in our lives where we are invited to cave in and stop expressing our true spirit. Try to retrieve these moments so they can be grieved, and thus healed.

Of course, these moments also occur as adults. We may date someone who bullies us, or work with a boss who devalues us to the point that we lose all self-respect. We may live in a country with a government that doesn't allow dissent. Or we may still be taking care of our family at the expense of our own hopes and dreams. Write down these observations, too; try to mine your life for every situation where you traded in your authenticity for some brand of people-pleasing. This is how your healing will begin; this is where your journey to authenticity starts.

DEFINING OUR CORE VALUES

Among the first steps to living a more authentic life is to really define, in detail, your core values. These can include compassion, kindness, honesty, belongingness, peacefulness, strength, healthiness, being in good physical shape, adventure, achievement, education, courage and bravery, love, culture, travel ... you name it; what matters is figuring out what really drives you in life and what you care about the most.

This process creates a tremendous amount of internal confidence because you will be able to hold every person, place, or thing up against your inner standard and say, "Does this match with my core values?" If it doesn't, then it's not right for you.

If one of your core values is peacefulness, for example, and you're dating someone who is constantly picking fights, you might have to face the fact that this relationship isn't serving your highest good. If one of your core values is creativity and you're sitting in a dead-end corporate job, it might be a wake-up call that it's time to search for more stimulating employment.

When we start to live by our core values rather than the values imposed on us by society, our family, our schools, or our jobs, our courage can have a ripple effect. Everyone we meet becomes emboldened and inspired by our authenticity. We see how we can make the most difference in the world just by being true to who and what we really are.

DISASSEMBLING OUR MASKS

Masks are the false selves we don to better survive or fit it. We all have them, to some degree, and learning to identify them—and release them—is an important leg of our journey towards greater authenticity.

An important aspect of masks to understand is that they tend to be one-dimensional, in that they only allow us to use a small portion of our personalities. They inhibit us by eliminating the full rainbow of possibilities that exists inside each of us. When we wear a mask, we have to be consistent and portray a false self with no cracks.

In reality, no one can ever be one hundred percent consistent. To be human means having a wide range of emotions and emotional states. Sometimes we're up and on our game, and sometimes we make mistakes. Sometimes we're very funny and engaging, and other times we can be shy and introverted.

Accepting and embracing all the parts of ourselves which have been locked away or forbidden is what becoming authentic means. It's about ceasing to control, censor, or repress, and simply welcoming the full spectrum that is us.

There is a lot of excellent literature on dysfunctional families and the roles that children end up playing in these situations. Among these are the Hero, the Enabler, the Lost Child, the Mascot, and the Scapegoat. These terms were first coined by psychologist Sharon Wegscheider-Cruse in 1981 (adapted from the work of Virginia Satir), and these terms describe the roles that help us to survive in childhood.

Unfortunately, these roles can persist into adulthood, where they become liabilities. Coping mechanisms that once sustained us become unsustainable and are in fact the source of much suffering. We will discuss each of these in some detail below; most of us fall into more than one category, suffering from some combination of all of them, so it's good to have an overview.

The Hero

The Hero is the mask worn by a child whose role it is to make the family appear functional and "normal." This child will often be a high achiever at school and will get good grades despite being under a lot of stress at home.

The Hero will have a perfectionist attitude towards everything they do and will be overly responsible and independent. From the outside, this person is often praised for their accomplishments and hard work and for never giving the family any problems.

But inside, the Hero will be hurting because they are not allowed to be human or to have off days. Their success will always be driven by others and a need to gain approval and be seen as "good." Thus, the Hero personality may end up suffering from stress-related illness, workaholism, or even addictions that help them maintain their high level of achievement. The ever-successful, brave, and strong persona is ultimately not sustainable because we are all only human.

The Hero has to slow down and learn to accept help from others. The Hero has to take off their mask and begin to get to know themselves and what they genuinely like doing with their time. In some ways, the Hero has quality problems because these people are often disciplined and organized. But they may not know how to have fun or relax, and they must learn these very human activities or risk depression and illness.

The Scapegoat

The Scapegoat, like its name implies, exists to bear the brunt of the family's dysfunction so that the adults can point to the child as "the problem" rather than focus on themselves. The Scapegoat child will have behavior issues, often acting out in defiance, anger, or hostility. They will be called rebellious and will be unable to stay out of conflict. These episodes will serve to distract outsiders from more serious underlying problems within the family. In this sense, the Scapegoat child has been sacrificed to maintain the family image.

Scapegoat children will have trouble in school, often getting poor grades and being punished. They know that they will always receive the most attention for screwing up, so they continue this behavior despite its negative consequences. The Scapegoat may be a leader within their group, but the people they choose to associate with are usually also delinquents of some kind, and thus can't offer true friendship or nurturing. As a result, the Scapegoat will be quite lonely.

Another incarnation of the Scapegoat is the child that is perpetually ill, sick, or weak. They may also be a child that is constantly bullied. Their weakness serves as a focal point on which the rest of the family can focus their attention, denying their own problems. This type of Scapegoat knows that they receive the most attention when they are sick, so they perpetually fail and under-achieve to continue getting this sort of backwards praise.

As adults, Scapegoats may find it hard to unravel the mystery of why they are struggling so much. It can be very painful to admit that one's family preferred us at our worst, during those times when we were in trouble or when we were weak and sick.

For this person, turning things around will mean owning their authentic talents and inner strength, which can feel like sabotage to the old family dynamics they have spent so long preserving. Scapegoats will need a lot of support to exchange their old ways for new, healthier expressions of their true capable, successful, and autonomous selves.

The Lost Child

A shy, dreamy, quiet personality will often be found with the Lost Child mask. This personality aims to be completely invisible and just melt into the woodwork, staying out of harm's way and simply spending all their time alone. They keep a low profile, to the degree that they are frequently forgotten or neglected.

The Lost Child doesn't cause any problems, and like with the Hero, the family can claim that nothing is wrong. But the Lost Child achieves this "goodness" by never interacting with anyone long enough to have a conflict. They are like ghosts that no one really knows. They are shy and withdrawn and can end up becoming socially and developmentally arrested because they are not taking the healthy risks required to grow and communicate. They may struggle their whole lives with intimate relationships and find it hard to get close to anyone.

Coming into greater authenticity for the Lost Child means owning their needs, wants, and desires. It means facing conflict and understanding that conflict is a healthy part of human intimacy. It means accepting that we are all interdependent and rely on one another for support and emotional nourishment. Making these changes can be challenging for the Lost Child, but it is possible to make that change, and a world of happiness awaits as they learn to trust others and let love in.

The Mascot

Also known as the "class clown" or "court jester," the Mascot's role is to give the family a break from its problems by making everybody laugh. This child may feel the extreme tension, anger, and conflict in the home, and want nothing more than to relieve it out of their own discomfort.

Mascots can be extraordinarily funny and charming and can entertain others for hours with their hilarious antics. In fact, they may end up making a living using their comedic abilities. They may be called cute, adorable, or the "baby" of the family. They may be habitually referred to as "nice;" everyone seems to like them and they will do anything to keep this image intact.

Underneath all this entertaining, however, the Mascot may struggle to communicate their feelings directly, instead relying on comedy or jokes to make their point. They may strive to constantly be on the go, putting on a show, and find it hard to spend time in solitude or be still. At heart, the Mascot is aiming to save their family from dysfunction and may retain this "savior role" as an adult in personal relationships.

To heal, the Mascot must begin to take themselves and their pain seriously. They must learn to balance their perpetual humor with self-reflection and know when to stop joking around and be real. The Mascot may also have to learn to put themselves first and stop trying to please others in life. This can be a rewarding journey of self-discovery and self-affirmation if they so choose.

The Enabler

Also referred to as "the caretaker," the Enabler has sacrificed their own needs to better attend to their dysfunctional family members. The Enabler feels responsible for keeping everyone happy and will take on responsibilities that shouldn't normally rest on a child's shoulders.

They are the family martyr. If a parent is sick, addicted, or mentally ill, the Enabler child may begin functioning as a surrogate guardian for the rest of the family. Their entire self-concept will be based on their ability to nurture, care for, listen to, counsel, and console their ailing relatives. The Enabler keeps the adults from having to own and face their own problems.

Enablers as adults face a particularly severe brand of codependence and must begin to dismantle it slowly. They have to learn to set healthy boundaries with others, not taking on more than their share of work, chores, or responsibilities. Just learning to say "no" is a major milestone.

Enablers must grieve the loss of their childhood adolescence when they had no time or energy to focus on themselves. Now, as adults, they must learn to take time to nourish themselves socially, romantically, professionally, and spiritually. Their path to authenticity will depend on to what degree they can let go of their self-image as savior and rescuer and simply enjoy the great things life has to offer them.

GENDER MASKS

Today, we are learning that gender is a far more fluid and malleable thing than we previously imagined. We are softening our expectations and learning to invite surprise and delight at what is possible for us as human beings.

We are learning to afford transgender, bigender, and genderqueer individuals the same rights and respect as cisgender folk experience. We may not know where all this acceptance is leading, but we can be sure we are moving in a more inclusive direction that prizes authenticity above conformity.

However, while gender identity may now be more flexible, many of us grew up with rigid stereotypes that caused us stress and internal conflict when we found we couldn't always conform.

Male Gender Identity

Boys are often raised to be "strong," which means never crying or showing their feelings. They are called "pussies," "sissies," or "fags" if they get too emotional. They may even risk being beaten up for being too "soft." Behind this is the idea of being a "soldier," someone who performs their duties with little or no emotional attachment.

Dealing with anger is also hard. Men are taught that it's more socially acceptable to be pissed off than to communicate hurt feelings, disappointment, or embarrassment. Violence may be sanctioned because it's considered superior to the possibility of letting others see the truth.

Of course, there is no such thing as a human being who doesn't have emotions or have a need to cry when they are sad. Suppressing one's sadness to appear brave can be devastating to one's health, physically, emotionally, and spiritually. Authenticity demands that we allow ourselves to be vulnerable and express our pain.

Additionally, boys may be raised to be "studs" and taught that aggressive hypersexuality is the norm. They may be encouraged to be womanizers or told that sexual expression is about acquire "conquests." This, together with peer pressure, creates an environment where male sexuality is all about notches on a belt and less about experiencing intimacy with a partner.

Men growing up with these internalized messages may struggle to form healthy relationships with the opposite sex. If gay, they may struggle with vulnerability and commitment. Learning about what constitutes authentic sexual identity can take time, because it means unlearning those entrenched ideas that helped us survive.

Boys and men must learn that they can be whimsical, sad, soft, teary-eyed, poetic, kind, caring, gentle, or quiet, and not have it bring their sexuality or gender identity into question. Learning to own all these qualities in oneself takes bravery and a big commitment to living an authentic life day by day. But it *is* possible, and today there is more safety and validation for an emotionally complex male identity than ever before.

Female Gender Identity

Of course, women suffer from stereotypes just as grievously, if not worse than their male counterparts. Due to sexism, women have had to disown their intelligence, their athleticism, their sex drive, their independence, their imagination, their leadership skills, and so many other amazing talents that they have to offer, all just to fit into a male-dominated paradigm that has been in place for hundreds of years.

Because women have been so devalued in the workplace and have experienced such bullying and such poor pay, many women feel they have had to compensate with hypersexuality, by flirting, intriguing, or otherwise going against our natural inclination for unadulterated ambition. We may have felt we had to put up with office come-ons or inappropriate behavior from our bosses just to keep our jobs.

As we have seen with the "me too" movement, all this is slowly changing. Women are learning that they can be everything they were born to be without having to "pay" for it through sexual favors, attention, or objectification.

As girls, many of us were raised to value our appearances over all other assets. This may have driven us to eating disorders, compulsive exercise, dieting, or taking pills, all to maintain an impossible image to please men and all while ignoring our secret desire to just be human.

As adults we may still find ourselves always worrying about being too fat, too old, too thin, too ugly, too tall, or too "something" to deserve love, respect, success, and happiness. This epidemic of self-hatred must end. We must learn to live in the deliciousness of really being who we are, *as is*. We can learn to celebrate our differences, our flaws, our uniqueness, and our idiosyncrasies as gifts rather than liabilities.

Women are also often traditionally cast as caregivers due to their maternal nature, and this can create a lot of problems for us in expressing authenticity. We may feel that others need us and rely on us, and we can't very well go and desert everyone to pursue our dreams.

What we need to learn to accept and believe is that everyone around us will actually be happier if we choose to live in authenticity. When we take care of ourselves by living in our truth rather than compulsively solving others' problems, we'll find everyone we come into contact with is affected positively. Rather than "selfishness," this healthy focus on our own goals helps us to live more in balance with others and help others to stand on their own two feet.

TOWARDS A MORE AUTHENTIC FUTURE

Moving towards greater authenticity means reassessing every area of our lives, from our choices in work and love, to our involvement in politics, religion, spirituality, and in community. It means refusing to take our roles or life scripts for granted, but rather investigating whether what we think about ourselves and where we belong is really valid.

How much of our lives have been dictated by our families, our governments, our teachers, or our peers? If we came from a neighborhood where everyone had tattoos and we got them, did we really want them? If we grew up in a family where everyone ate a lot of meat, do we really enjoy eating meat, or do we eat it because it's the status quo for our "tribe?" If we've chosen to be independent and driven in our career, did we make this choice to rebel against our mother's dependency and lack of autonomy? How many of our choices in life are reactions, rather than authentic actions?

There are a million and one variations on this question, and asking them can be exciting. Uncovering the real version of ourselves—as compared to the canned, auto-pilot version—can be a joyous revelation. As each of us commits to more and more authenticity, our world becomes a more colorful, bright, and magical place.

Taking the Next Step

On the next page, you will find twenty affirmations on the topic of building greater authenticity in your life. You can use these however you see fit; just by reading them right now, you are beginning to shift your mind and heart towards a more genuine expression of your being.

Affirmations for Authenticity

- I am the architect of my own life.
- I am perfect exactly as I am.
- Today, I will embrace my uniqueness and allow myself to shine.
- Every day, I grow to like myself more and more.
- I am confident in who I am.
- I let go easily of that which no longer suits me.
- I release unsupportive relationships from my life.
- My actions are now aligned with my deepest values and beliefs.
- It is safe to be myself around others.
- I take the time to get to know myself fully.
- I feel at ease in my own skin.
- I am worthy of having good things in my life.
- I don't have to prove my worth to others; I have worth simply because I exist.
- I measure my success by the peace within me.
- I have no need to compare myself to others.
- There is enough time, love and money.
- I am generous with my time, money and love.
- I release all self-doubt and move steadily toward my life's purpose.
- I let go of all physical tension and breathe deeply.
- I am whole and I am healed.

Chapter 3

SELF-CARE

"I have come to believe that caring for myself is not self-indulgent. Caring for myself is an act of survival."

—Audre Lorde

Self-care is a broad topic, grouping many elements under a single umbrella. Learning to balance each of these areas individually can be a challenge all on its own, so it's useful to explore each motif separately before combining them all to create the rich, thriving experience that is being alive.

The term "self-care" includes (but is not limited to):

- eating properly
- exercising
- sleeping well
- coping appropriately with stress, shame, grief and disappointment
- socializing

- dating

- healthy solitude

- spirituality

- relaxation and rest

- practicing gratitude

- taking care of financial matters

- meeting obligations

…and so many other important daily rituals of mindfulness.

Although this list is by no means comprehensive, we will explore each of these elements in this chapter, creating a basic blueprint for a more expansive, fulfilling lifestyle.

Self-care can be difficult for those that never received nurturing from their primary caretakers. After all, it's nearly impossible to receive love when we do not care to love ourselves. There can be a lot of grief and surrender involved in finally taking responsibility for your own well-being when no one else has loved you properly in so long. But with each act of self-love, and as the Universe moves in to support your intentions, you will find that more loving, nourishing relationships begin to blossom.

Self-care can be roughly divided into six categories: mental self-care, emotional self-care, physical self-care, spiritual self-care, social self-care, and financial self-care.

MENTAL SELF-CARE

Dealing with Stress

Stress is one of the major risk factors for illness. Most people are aware of this at some level, though few understand the degree to which this is the case. Working to reduce stress in your life can pay huge dividends in terms of saved time, saved money, improved health, and better relationships. Best of all, it can create a more peaceful, comfortable mental environment.

Proper nutrition. This may be the mental self-care section, but all aspects of self-care are connected, so the most obvious place to begin managing mental stress is with your body, through diet and exercise.

The most common major stressors on our body are caffeine, alcohol, nicotine, and sugar. We turn to these substances as a shortcut to dealing with stress, but over time, they become their own liabilities, putting strain on our organs and inhibiting a peaceful frame of mind.

Finding healthy substitutes for these products can be an adventure, but we now have so many new alternatives such as items made with cacao (raw chocolate), green tea, agave, dates, coconut, etc. that taste delicious while sparing our bodies the toxicity. Finding replacements for these substances may take some creativity and getting used to, but ultimately your body—and mind—will thank you.

Getting active. Engaging in physical activity may be the last thing on your mind when you're stressed out; however, since stress releases hormones such as adrenaline and cortisol, getting moving can help trick your body into believing it has successfully executed a "fight or flight" response, which in turn causes it to dial down the stress. Even though it might seem overly simple, going for a brisk walk when you feel tense can do wonders for your mood and mental state.

Practicing assertiveness. Another important method of dealing with stress is to work on assertiveness. So often when we're faced with a problem or conflict, we cower or retreat because we lack the skills needed to successfully navigate the situation. This, in turn, causes us an excess of mental stress.

Learning how to stand up for yourself and express your opinions and beliefs while still respecting others can go a long way in creating harmonious relationships with coworkers, bosses, friends, and family members.

Assertiveness is *not* the same thing as being dominating or demanding. It simply means standing strong in your core opinions and not backing down because you're too afraid to rock the boat. Assertiveness can lead to win-win scenarios, which are always the best for everyone involved.

Ask yourself: do you take on more responsibilities than you're able to carry just to please others? Do you keep silent when important matters are being discussed and then resent others' decisions later? Do you judge or blame others before talking things over? Do you use "I" statements rather than using accusatory language? Do you know how to say "no?"

Is your body language communicating confidence and security, or are you afraid to make eye contact? Are you slouching or hiding? Does your face properly communicate what you're feeling in the moment? Do you breathe and get centered before speaking? Is your voice calm, yet authoritative enough for others to take you seriously? Working on assertiveness can go a long way in minimizing the stress you feel in otherwise stress-inducing situations.

Time management. Practicing effective time management is one the major keys to reducing mental stress. Having an overwhelming, constantly revolving to-do list seems a normal feature of busy urban life, but perpetual busyness can take a huge toll on our quality of life.

Try to organize your list with the things that are genuine priorities at the top, followed by the less important things, and finally the items that can be postponed without ill effects. Also, organize your list by the things that you must do on your own, and then those items that could be successfully delegated to others.

There are also several effective habits you can cultivate to use your time more effectively. For example, creating a buffer for arrival and departures is part of effective time management. If you commit to arriving at every appointment fifteen to twenty minutes early, you will be amazed by how much mental stress is relieved. Not to mention, if you're early to everything, people will appreciate you more than words can say. You may even find yourself promoted at work for being the most reliable and punctual person at your office.

Similarly, at the end of the work day or at the end of an event, schedule in "wrapping up" time. It always takes longer than you might think to extricate yourself from conversations and tasks. Let others know your boundaries with time by saying such things as, "I have to wrap up in about ten minutes, just to warn you," or, "I'm planning to get going in around fifteen minutes." This helps others to adjust, and you might even get a reply like, "Okay, I won't keep you," or, "I know you're trying to get out of here." Everyone deals with the same stressors; they will understand your desire to keep to your schedule!

Achieving Balance

Living a balanced life means making time for rest and relaxation, socializing, dating, romance, exercise, meditation, reading, earning, making art, and all the other activities that are integral to being human. When we start to prioritize one activity, such as working, sleeping, or romance, to the detriment of all other activities, it can create a lot of mental strain.

Addiction itself is based on excess or deprivation of some kind, so a common element of any recovery program is to work on detecting when one is in danger of approaching imbalance and trying to course-correct. Becoming aware of the areas of our life where excess dwells and where there is a lack helps us to take the necessary actions for a balanced life.

Creating balance also requires constant adjustment. Unforeseen circumstances arise, emergencies come up, plans get rearranged; nothing is set in stone, but having a rough pie chart of how you want to spend your time is a good idea. When you get it down on paper, you may be surprised by what you see.

If you feel your life is out of balance, why not start with just balancing today? How can you structure the next twenty-four hours to reflect more of a balanced lifestyle? Can you exercise for fifteen minutes? Catch up with a friend for twenty minutes? Work on your screenplay for ten minutes? Take a hot bath for thirty minutes? These small, attainable goals can help you feel that you're "getting it all in," which brings a feeling of mental satisfaction as we see progress in all areas.

Slowing Down

This is a big one. Our world races along at such a terrifyingly rapid pace these days, we all feel the need to keep up, to rush, to be super productive, and to get ahead. What we don't realize is that in doing so, we're sacrificing the deep joy of being in the present moment, just accepting everything exactly as it is and taking time to "smell the roses."

Taking a pause during our day to just enjoy the scenery, engage with an animal, or read some jokes online can do wonders for our mental state. It's so important to take life with a grain of salt and just detach a little bit when things feel out of control.

Slowing down doesn't mean reneging on our responsibilities, either. It just means inserting some downtime into our day so we can renew and recharge. It means creating little rituals we enjoy that can help to balance the stress of modern urban living.

Can you take a moment to breathe in and out deeply, allowing yourself to connect with your environment? Can you make yourself a nice hot cup of tea and savor it? Can you take a moment to talk to a child and let them tell you a knock-knock joke? Can you pause to smile at a stranger? These small actions can help create tremendous space in your life and a more open, positive mental climate.

Taking Naps

The phrase "taking a nap" may cause you to flashback to kindergarten, or it may cause you to flash forward to old age. But children and seniors are not the only ones who can use a good nap! Taking naps throughout the day is an excellent way to recharge your mind at any age. A quick twenty- to thirty-minute nap can totally reboot your brain and help you to be productive and alert for the rest of the day. There is absolutely no shame in just lying down and shutting your eyes and letting sleep take over. And it's far superior to opting for energy drinks or caffeine when you're feeling depleted.

Keeping Mentally Active

Just like the body, the brain requires regular exercise in order to stay fit. As we get older, our brains can stagnate just like our muscles, so we have to keep in shape by engaging in mentally stimulating activities such as reading, taking classes, playing strategic games, doing crossword puzzles, or joining in political debates.

Keeping mentally active can help ward off depression and boredom, as well as loneliness. It can help spice up a routine job and can also work to ward off memory loss or dementia as one gets older.

EMOTIONAL SELF-CARE

Working with a Professional

There is a trend in the American collective consciousness toward self-sufficiency that, while empowering on one level, can keep us from seeking out the help we need when we're in pain or struggling. Far more common—and realistic—than the myth of the man pulling himself up by his bootstraps is the story of the person who received support, networking, nurturing, friendship, and favors from those around him and thus was able to succeed.

There is absolutely no shame in getting assistance with your life, especially for your emotional health. Seeing a therapist or psychiatrist once a week can create a safe space to process difficult feelings confidentially. You might also choose to work with a life coach, someone you trust who can help you deal with the ups and downs of living in increasingly complex times.

The wonderful thing about living in our current era is that there are dozens of therapeutic mediums to choose from, ranging from psychodrama to art therapy. Not everyone will respond to talk therapy, so don't worry if it doesn't appeal to you. Try to find a different kind that appeals to your personality.

Body Work

While one might initially think that body work (massage, reiki, Feldenkrais, rolfing) would be in the section for physical self-care, I have listed it here because of the tremendous emotional release that body work can provide. We store our emotions in our bodies, and when we receive a therapeutic touch, it can heal us from an unexpected perspective.

There are many types of body work, the most common being massage. And there are many types of massage, from deep tissue to Hawaiian to sports massage. Receiving therapeutic, non-sexual touches from a professional can help us to feel less lonely and more connected. Just as babies need to be held or they will perish, as adults, we also need touch in order to be emotionally grounded, secure, and at peace.

Keeping a Journal

Writing down our feelings in a diary is an excellent way to get in touch with ourselves and better know our own minds. Try writing at least three pages a day in your journal for thirty days. At the end of the month, read your entries and see if you find any trends. What is bothering you the most, according to your writing? What gives you the most peace and joy? What makes you laugh?

As an example, it can be a revelation to read your own writing about wanting to leave a job you dislike. Seeing it there in black and white makes it very real, and it's impossible not to take action and move forward when your own voice is telling you to let go.

Learning Communication Skills

You may not realize it, but good communication skills are not something we're always born with. Some of us have to learn and practice it, just like we would an instrument. The key behaviors that support healthy communication are: being present and active listening, body language, practicing empathy, getting clarity, providing appropriate feedback, and creating a sense of trust. Understanding these elements allows us to express our emotions with much more confidence and better understand others' emotions.

Being present. Being present means putting down the phone, turning off the TV, taking out the headphones, and actually making eye contact. Active listening is about listening with your whole body, reading in between the lines, and extracting the essence of someone's message to you from their tone of voice, their facial expression, and the energy they are projecting.

Body language. Are you aware of how you communicate nonverbally? A compassionate handshake or tap on the shoulder can send a signal of security and friendship beyond words. Do you fold your arms across your chest to put up a barrier? Or do you leave your palms turned upwards in a gesture of openness and receiving? There are so many ways that we communicate with each other without words, and being mindful of these practices can help us to improve the connection we make with others.

Practicing empathy. Practicing empathy is a choice when communicating. We can choose to relate to another's feelings and experiences, rather than focusing on what we *don't* have in common with the person.

Getting clarity. Getting clarity by asking questions helps us to get all the facts before reacting. So often, we tend to jump the gun and respond to someone before we've fully assessed the situation, with disastrous results. Insisting on being clear with others helps them to understand us better. Clarity may even include stating that you don't know the answer. As long as you are honest, others will appreciate your efforts.

Providing appropriate feedback. Providing healthy feedback to others is an important element of communication. It's not about ripping someone apart with criticism, but about acknowledging both the good things and the things that need to be worked on. Everyone on the planet likes to be thanked for their efforts and appreciated.

Creating a sense of trust. The exact method involved in creating a sense of trust will be unique to every individual, but it generally involves honesty, keeping your word, being reliable, and being accountable. Trust is based on the repetition of positive actions. Every day we see the sun rise, so we trust that tomorrow it will happen again. Being consistent with others is an excellent way to establish a healthy pattern of shared trust and communication.

PHYSICAL SELF-CARE

Exercising

There is nothing more important for a healthy life than exercise. The body requires exercise just as it requires water. Without it, the mind and body begin to atrophy, depression and anxiety ensue, and one just cannot be as productive, healthy, and happy as we are meant to be.

For many people, the problem is that they have a hard time finding exercise that they enjoy doing. It's so easy to try one thing, hate it, and then never go back to the gym. Luckily, the world of exercise is vast, with as many types of physical activities as there are people! There is snowshoeing, hang gliding, line dancing, volleyball, ping pong, tennis, basketball, gymnastics, yoga, hot yoga, ballet, tap dancing, hand ball, parkour, jumping rope, boxing, martial arts, surfing, swimming, water aerobics, weight lifting ... and that's just the tip of the iceberg.

Find something you enjoy doing that gets you moving, and commit to doing it a few times a week, imperfectly or otherwise. Be like a detective, and don't stop trying different activities until you find the one that works for your life. Exercise is truly meant to be fun, not a chore or a punishment. If you take a look at any little kid, they're not "exercising"—they're just moving their bodies for pleasure, and this is the feeling we want to recapture as adults.

Another aspect of exercise is that it doesn't take as much as you think to help get the endorphins going. Even just a fifteen-minute brisk walk around your neighborhood is enough to produce a positive mood and outlook. The blood starts flowing, circulation improves, and your body begins to say thank you in small, perceptible ways.

Eating Well

While some people use food as recreation, ultimately the food we put in our bodies is responsible for the lives we lead. It is our fuel and energy to perform the important tasks of living, and as such, it must be efficient and enriching.

Food can be a battleground for classism and elitism, as many "healthy" stores charge exorbitant prices while paying their employees so little that they can't afford to shop where they work. It's important to remember that health belongs to everyone, regardless of economic status. Health is a human right. So, if your local supermarket doesn't stock organic produce, perhaps it's time for them to start doing so—at a reasonable price.

It may also be tempting to think of healthy eating as a fad. While many companies take advantage of health fads and special fancy diets, these are usually not sustainable in the end. What *is* sustainable is eating a balanced diet of proteins, starches, and fats, and keeping processed foods, alcohol, and caffeine to a minimum. Being too rigid or too strict with one's diet is a set-up for negative excess when the pendulum swings the other way. It's better to adopt simple, easy-to-follow eating habits that are generally healthy without being too extreme.

Sleeping Well

Treating ourselves to a good night's sleep is a decision we must make each day, and it requires some attention, since it doesn't always just happen naturally. The quality and quantity of our sleep determines how we feel, the work we get done, our interactions with others, and our outlook on life for the day.

It is therefore essential that we create a routine for getting the best night's rest. This may include winding down an hour before bedtime, drinking a soothing cup of herbal tea, taking a hot bath, or reading a book in bed. These practices signal the brain that it's time to relax and release the events of the day. Listening to affirmations or audio recordings can also be a great way to let go of our worries and start to drift off.

You can also investigate your sleeping arrangements if you're having trouble getting to bed. Ask yourself, "Do I enjoy my bed? Is it comfortable? Do I need to invest in a better mattress? What about my pillow? Is it too soft or too hard? Do I have pajamas? Do I have the right lighting for sleep?" All these considerations can be adjusted to create the perfect environment for a good night's rest to occur.

Dressing for Success

How we present ourselves to the world in terms of our appearance matters deeply. We are primarily a visual culture, and the sense of sight is dominant in our brains. Practicing excellent grooming and hygiene is essential for success, both socially and professionally. It's not about looking like someone you're not, but about putting your best foot forward in life by taking the time to select a wardrobe that boosts your self-esteem.

When was the last time you went shopping for new clothes or new shoes? When did you last have a haircut or get a professional shave? If you're going out for a job interview, can you imagine how impressive it might be to review a candidate who is wearing a fantastic outfit and looks the part? If you're going out on a date, why not really put effort and time into dressing up?

So often, we're afraid others will laugh at us or judge us if we change or seek to improve our appearances, but looking good can go a long way in shaping a positive self-image, itself a foundation for healthy living. So don't be afraid to take a risk and express your personal style!

Healing from Addictions

Today, more so than at any time in history, addiction can be treated, managed, and healed. There is an unprecedented amount of community support for those suffering from substance abuse issues, food addiction, nicotine addiction, self-harming, sex addiction ... the list goes on. Making the decision to face a debilitating addiction can be difficult, but there is no greater act of self-love.

Today, addiction is seen as illness, rather than a moral failing. This is a new paradigm from the old days when addicts were shamed, ostracized, stigmatized, and cast out. For today's addict, a regimen of self-care and self-love is the goal for recovery, and this is understood to be a gentle process that doesn't happen overnight. It's a commitment to meeting one's needs for affection, recreation, rest, creative and professional fulfillment, and intimacy in a healthy, new way, and this takes patience.

SPIRITUAL SELF-CARE

Spending Time in Solitude

No life can be peaceful and productive without adequate time spent in solitude. We require it, just like we require sleep. It can be very hard to come by, especially when you're a parent or juggling multiple jobs where you're constantly in the presence of others. But to keep our souls nourished and nurtured, spending quality time alone is mandatory.

If you are the type of person who is always running from yourself and never wants to be alone, you might question why this is the case. Sometimes, it's just because we haven't really met ourselves yet or haven't taken the time to get to know ourselves. Once we do, however, we usually find that the feelings we feared most are not life-threatening, as we feared. It is quite enjoyable to find refuge in the depth of our own soul; to walk inwards and meet ourselves is one of life's great joys.

It's been said that the world extends infinitely inwards just as it extends infinitely outwards. In other words, there is just as much to explore inside us as there is in outer space.

Spending time in solitude also lets us strengthen our intuition. The more we are able to quiet down and truly listen to our intuition, the more it comes to our aid in everyday life. It is a muscle, and it requires flexing.

We can ask questions of the Universe and hear them answered when we're quiet and alone. If we're constantly filling our minds with film, TV, social media, conversations, texts, apps, the internet, and entertainment, there isn't much room to connect with our highest selves and our creativity. We end up feeling a spiritual void, and this leads to depression, anxiety, and existential malaise, none of which is truly necessary to leading a fulfilling and balanced life.

Spending Time in Nature

As human beings, we need sunshine and fresh air to feel alive. Our feet crave to feel the soil and the sand, and our eyes long to gaze upon the sunrise, the stars. Our soul thirsts for the sound of the ocean and the howl of the wind. We *need* these interactions to feel connected and grounded on the planet, and when we starve ourselves of contact with nature, we start to pay the price mentally, physically, emotionally, and spiritually.

As we spend more and more time as a society looking at screens, we dissociate from that primal connection to Mother Earth. Connecting with nature helps us to place ourselves within a context. We see how we are tiny, vulnerable beings in a grand cosmos. Our egos slip away as we surrender to our rightful place in the Universe.

This also leads to a feeling of gratitude for this planet, which is our only home. When we take time to truly enjoy the waterfalls, rainbows, landscapes, and sunsets of planet Earth, it gives us a deep motivation to practice green living and be mindful of the impact we make here on the planet.

Meditation

It cannot be overstated how integral the practice of meditation is to a healthy, balanced, emotionally stable life. Meditation cultivates a conscious connection with our highest selves, with the Universe, and with our intuition. It is the time in our day where we get to ask questions and receive answers in silence, ruminating on the important issues in our lives and how to solve them.

Mediation can help tremendously with anxiety. It stills our minds and helps us to focus on our breathing, becoming more present and in the moment. If we practice meditation often enough, eventually we find ourselves carrying this calm, centered frame of mind into all areas of life, whether we're locked in heavy traffic, on the phone with an irate client, or dealing with unruly teenagers at home. We find ourselves able to cope with challenges in a more peaceful, positive manner, and this is a huge gift.

Meditation is also a time when we get to stop running away from our emotions and problems and face ourselves squarely, resolutely accepting whatever we are feeling. Having the courage to be alone with ourselves in silence is one of the most empowering activities there is. It is the essence of self-acceptance, which leads to greater acceptance of others.

Prayer

While many of us choose to recite formal prayers as part of a religious tradition, prayer can still be a part of life for those that don't subscribe to conventional views. A prayer is simply a request for aid or an expression of gratitude. A prayer can be worded in any way; so long as it is genuine, it has great power and weight. Prayers can be said for oneself, for loved ones, for pets, or for the whole world. There are no rules when it comes to praying; it is an action that makes us feel connected and humble, and that in itself is worthwhile.

Practicing Gratitude

Health experts have confirmed that an attitude of gratitude is the most salient feature of those that have recovered from serious illnesses. Gratitude is literally a healing force, one that can change your life. Gratitude is a choice we make each day, beginning with the moment we wake up. It is a choice to focus on what we *do* have, what *is* working, what *is* going right in our world, all the people that help and support us, and all the abundance we have on Earth.

If you are struggling with gratitude, challenge yourself to make a list of 100 things to be grateful for. As you go down your list, notice if your whole mood and outlook begins to soften and improve. It's simply impossible to practice gratitude without smiling from ear to ear. It uplifts and renews us, even in times of great sorrow and struggle. After you make your list, continue to make a daily list of ten items every day for thirty days.

Being Kind

Being kind, like practicing gratitude, is a choice we make each day when we wake up. The decision to be kind to all those we encounter throughout our day can really create a new experience of common challenges such as navigating traffic, dealing with homeless people, or dealing with customer service representatives. There is nothing more wonderful than having a stranger smile at you or hearing a kind word when you're doing your job, so why not be the person supplying the kindness? This world is hard enough, and everyone, absolutely everyone, needs love and support. From animals to senior citizens, children and adults of all ages, we all enjoy a friendly gesture, a pat on the back, a random gift; these small kindnesses are what make us human!

SOCIAL SELF-CARE

You may be doing everything right for yourself in terms of nutrition, exercise, sleep, and spirituality, but as human beings, we thrive on social interaction. We are social creatures, and if we aren't socializing on a regular basis, we may feel ill—socially ill—even within an otherwise healthy body.

Having Fun

Having fun is mandatory for a healthy life! It may seem common sense, but when was the last time you really had fun? If you can't answer that question, it's time to start dedicating part of your day, every day, to having a little fun. Whether it's playing a joke on a colleague at work or going to karaoke for a half hour, put in the effort to pack in the fun!

Many of us grew up in households where fun was frowned upon and we were punished for even trying to have fun. This changes *today*. No matter how old you are, try to recapture that childlike sense of fun that is innate in every one of us. With even just ten minutes of fun a day, you may see remarkable improvement in your mood and your entire outlook on life!

Dating

Dating comes easily to some folks, but there are others that find this area of life particularly challenging. If it's hard for you to put yourself out there and date, you are not alone. Dating can bring up incredible vulnerability and old wounds, so it's normal to want to avoid it completely if you've been through any sort of trauma in your life. But as human beings, we thrive on partnership and intimacy, and everyone deserves the love and support that relationships bring.

If you have been putting off dating, try thinking of it more as a tool of self-care, and as an expression of self-love. Remove the importance placed on results and shift the emphasis on you and your actions. It doesn't matter how others respond; what matters is that you are doing something loving for yourself by reaching out and inviting romance into your life. The Universe will surely see your bravery and meet you halfway.

There are lots of great dating apps out there today that target a healthy lifestyle, including meetmindful.com, which allows you to meet other people who are into eating healthy food, doing yoga, practicing green living, and much more. There are also websites for particular lifestyles, including musician dating, vegetarian dating, dating over fifty, and many others. If you hate online dating, take a look at the singles events available in your area. The key is to have the willingness to open up to new possibilities. Dating *can* actually be fun if you keep your expectations low and your sense of adventure high!

Joining a Community

We all need community. Yet today, more than at any other point in history, we have become so independent that it *is* possible to live without actually interacting with anyone in person. You can order everything you need online and have it dropped in your mailbox; you can work from home on the computer; you can communicate with anyone, anywhere, without seeing their face.

All this incredible technology has made us more fragmented as a culture, and our instincts to be part of a tribe are repressed. So, since it doesn't necessarily come naturally anymore, we have to take action to seek out community in our lives. We can do this in any number of ways: by joining a local sports team, finding a meditation group, attending church, joining a book club, or participating in the parent-teacher association. Feeling like you're part of something, feeling included and connected, are emotions that are integral to a happy, purposeful life.

Adopting a Rescue Dog

If you've ever had a dog, then you know firsthand the boundless love and affection that man's best friend can bring to our lives. Dogs show us a kind of loyalty and unconditional acceptance that we may never have experienced from humans. They delight us, entertain us, and fill us with childlike wonder. They help us to be less selfish and care for another living being that depends on us. They brighten our days and cuddle us at night.

In short, dogs are *the best*! And so many of them are just waiting for their forever homes in a shelter or rescue. Getting a dog can be one of the best decisions of your life, especially if you struggle with loneliness or commitment issues.

Giving Back

I believe wholeheartedly that part of being a happy, healthy human being is giving back to others. Wherever you are in your life, there are others less fortunate that you can help. Getting out of your own head and into the spirit of generosity and gratitude can do wonders for your mental outlook.

You can feed the homeless, hold babies at the hospital, volunteer to tutor disadvantaged kids, or assist new entrepreneurs through SCORE, an agency that matches retired business owners with those just starting out. It doesn't really matter what you choose; the idea is just to get out there and give of your time, energy, and love. The more we give that stuff away, the more it redoubles in our own lives.

FINANCIAL SELF-CARE

The last piece of our self-care puzzle is the financial side of things. Whether we like it or not, money is a sort of energy that we must exchange with others on a daily basis. Many of us received a lot of unhealthy messages about money as children. We might have felt like a burden to our parents financially, or we might have received money as a substitute for love. We may have grown up believing that "the rich don't go to heaven," or alternatively, that we should use credit cards to fund a lifestyle beyond our means.

Working through our issues with money takes time and commitment, but it can be done with support and dedication. Being financially healthy doesn't necessarily mean being wealthy, either; it just means having a good relationship with our income, our debts, our cash flow, and our recordkeeping—in other words, being at peace around our finances.

Working with a Financial Professional

There are individuals who have no problem seeing a therapist for their relationships, yet who have never considered seeing a financial advisor to help them with their money. In this life, we need all the help we can get, so why not consider going to a professional for financial guidance? Finding out now rather than later what you need to save for retirement, finding out everything you need to know about taxes, or finding out how to invest or buy a home are all great steps to monetary self-care.

Dealing with Creditors

In today's society, nearly all of us have debt: student loan debt, debt to the IRS, credit card debt, or personal debt to friends and family. Debt is a difficult cross to bear, but it needn't ruin your life. The reality is that many creditors are willing to make payment arrangements or even to forgive a portion of your debt. It simply requires facing them and negotiating. The more you bury your head in the sand, the worse things get. If you need extra support, you can always attend your local Debtors Anonymous meeting, a program of recovery around compulsive debting, spending, and shopping.

Keeping Financial Records

One of the best ways to get and maintain clarity on your finances is to keep daily records of everything you spend and everything you earn. There are several good phone apps that do this, including Billguard, Dollarbird, and Mint. At the end of the month, you can add up the daily totals for all the different categories, including food, shelter, clothing, entertainment, education, etc., and enter them into Excel or another money-tracking software.

This kind of recordkeeping can give you a more accurate picture of your finances than what you may have been imagining. For instance, you might be surprised to see on paper that you're spending upwards of $50 a week at Starbucks—money that you could be saving for a vacation. Recordkeeping gives you the clarity to make decisions about how, when, and where you spend your cash.

Starting a Business

Starting a business is the American Dream for many people, yet it can be daunting to even think about. There is so much to consider, from start-up costs to marketing and advertising to whether or not to hire staff.

Fortunately, for almost any business you can imagine starting, there are people who have done it before and who are willing to help. SCORE is an organization that provides small business counseling at no cost to members of the community and is a great place to start your journey. Wisebread.com provides an easy-to-answer four-question business plan that will get you thinking in the right direction about your target audience, your competitors, and your marketing strategy.

Starting a business can be a huge source of pride and accomplishment and may also provide you with financial freedom and more flexible working hours. Don't be discouraged by the thought of all the hard work. Instead, be open and willing to receive support from friends, family, a Kickstarter, SCORE, and many other avenues that may open up once you decide you're willing to pursue your dreams.

Remember that, while owning a business can sometimes breed uncertainty, nine-to-five jobs are also uncertain, as they leave you at the whim of an employer. Uncertainty is simply a part of life in all areas and is only an obstacle if you let it deter you. You are of the most service to others when you're out there doing what you absolutely love—so don't delay!

Finding a Job You Love

Our health depends on many factors, but one of these you may not commonly consider is joy. If you are miserable at your job, you are not doing anyone any favors. You may end up having stress-related illnesses, boredom, depression, anxiety, or any other number of symptoms all from hating your line of work.

You may be frightened to leave a miserable job for the unknown, but at the end of the day, there may be no good reason other than fear for why you can't go back to school to get a new skill, train for a new profession, start a business, or start doing something you're naturally good at and just never tried to earn from before.

Tremendous joy takes tremendous risk, but the payoffs are worth it. If you're not sure where to begin, there is a wonderful book called *What Color is Your Parachute?* by Dick Bolles that provides insight on choosing a new career that's right for you.

Taking the Next Step

We end this chapter by providing you with twenty affirmations you can use on a daily basis to improve your self-care and move past blockages that are preventing you from experiencing total joy, peace, and productivity. You can read these out loud, print them and hang them in your room, or glance at them whenever you see fit. Trust that they are already working in your life this very minute as you make your way through this book.

Affirmations for Self-Care

- I handle stress with ease and rise to the occasion.
- I practice assertiveness and speak up for myself with ease.
- I slow down and take time to smell life's roses.
- I allow myself to get proper rest and relaxation.
- I find it easy to ask others for help when I need it most.
- I communicate clearly and effectively with others.
- Today, I choose to put only nutritious, healthy foods into my body.
- Today, I choose to present myself in the most attractive manner possible.
- I release the need to numb my feelings.
- I spend time in solitude, connecting deeply with my inner voice.
- I embrace nature and lose myself in beauty.
- I breathe in love and I breathe out joy.
- I am grateful for all the good in my life.
- Today, I will have some fun and enjoy myself.
- I am willing to take risks to meet new people.
- My heart is open and I am ready for love.
- Today I will take the time to care for my finances.
- I am learning new things every day, growing and evolving effortlessly.
- I am effortlessly opening up to new possibilities for earning.
- I love my work and I am handsomely rewarded for my efforts.

Chapter 4

NUTRITION

"The food you eat can be either the safest and most powerful form of medicine or the slowest form of poison."

—ANN WIGMORE

Practicing good nutrition is essential to leading a healthy life. What we put in our bodies affects us for the hours, weeks, months, and years that follow, impacting our moods, our outlook, our energy levels, our muscles and bones, our skin, our teeth, our eyesight, our stamina, our sex drives, our weight, and our freedom from—or surrender to—diseases such as cancer, diabetes, osteoporosis, hypertension, and heart disease.

Today, more people are ill and obese than ever before, due in large part to unhealthy eating habits and a rise in fast food and processed foods. With our busy lifestyles, people spend less time cooking and less time eating with friends and family. Eating is done quickly, in the car or on the go, which is not good for our digestion.

What's worse, eating healthy has become seen as something for the elite, something only possible for those who can afford to shop at Whole

Foods or other fancy health food stores. Fast food joints open new branches in poor neighborhoods, preying on those who can't afford to buy organic vegetables and fresh produce. You may even feel like "eating healthy" is just another trend, instead of the life-and-death issue that it actually is.

By reading this book, you've already proven that you care for yourself. Now it's time to appreciate how learning to adopt a healthy, balanced diet is another important step towards self-love. Respecting our bodies by providing them with natural, unprocessed foods and enough water and vitamins should be viewed as a show of gratitude for the privilege of having a body that works and functions properly in the first place.

Anyone who has even been through a serious health scare, whether with cancer, heart disease, or diabetes, can tell you how it changed their outlook in a hurry. But why wait for such a serious wake-up call? Why not simply make today the start of a newly conscious and mindful lifestyle, paying more attention to what you eat and drink? The benefits this approach will bring in terms of happiness, usefulness, productivity, and improved relationships are well worth it.

PERSONAL NARRATIVES AROUND NUTRITION

I've encountered many clients who know everything there is to know about nutrition, yet remain stuck, unable to change their diets or to lose weight. For them, it's not a matter of lacking knowledge or understanding; rather, it is a psychological component such as fear, mistrust, or sadness that must be resolved in order to heal.

One of the greatest obstacles to losing weight occurs when we come from a family of overeaters. Losing weight can be seen as a betrayal of the core family identity. The skinny one might even be seen as a traitor ("Who does she think she is?") This can be a terrifying dynamic to overcome, and working through the intensity of these issues might benefit from the loving support of a therapist.

Other times, we fail to eat properly out of spite towards an over-controlling parent. Food is a battleground in many homes, a means of control and manipulation. Feeding a child, normally a loving act of nurturing, can become an act of dominance and ownership. Family dinners might have been the scene of fights or bickering, instead of the picturesque communing seen in Norman Rockwell paintings. Is it any wonder, then, that a child who grew up in such an environment where food was linked to abuse would struggle with self-care around proper nutrition?

What is your personal narrative with eating and food? Were you neglected as a kid, and now follow a rigid food plan just to feel some structure in your life? Or were you forced to repress your anger and rage, stuffing down your feelings by eating everything in sight? Did you starve yourself so you wouldn't have to feel your feelings? Or did you comfort yourself in the face of social rejection by indulging in the one thing in life that brought you pleasure?

All of these stories are perfectly normal and understandable. But today marks the turning of the page, a new chapter in our lives where we get to choose our own relationship with food, unaffected by society, our parents, our peers, our coworkers, our siblings, or our lovers. We get to design a plan of eating and nutrition that suits our lifestyle, appeals to our senses, delights us, and keeps us healthy, happy, and energized.

LEARNING TO COOK AND PREPARE FOOD

If you are truly seeking to improve your diet and your health, then learning to cook and prepare your own meals can be one of the most empowering and rewarding actions you can take towards your goal.

If you've never cooked before and have always just purchased your food on the go, it can seem daunting to adopt a brand-new skill set. But it's not as hard as you might think: just about anyone can learn to make healthy salads, stir-fries, delicious pasta dishes, and more. It just takes a little patience, a little willingness, and a small sense of adventure.

There are many easy recipes you can try, and once you find a few dishes you really enjoy, you will start looking forward to making your own meals. There are also many instructional videos you can watch and follow on YouTube and on television intended for the new, aspiring chef. Cooking for oneself is also an excellent way to stay on top of the ingredients you use, especially if you are trying to avoid items such as added sugars, extra salt, MSG, and the like.

SHOPPING FOR FRUITS AND VEGETABLES

Selecting the freshest, tastiest fruits and vegetables is a skill one develops over time. When you're just starting out, it's always a great idea to ask shopkeepers or farmers for advice. They are usually excited to help you select just the right veggies for your needs.

The following guide can also help shed some light on the process:

FRUITS

Apples. The best apples are firm to the touch, have a shiny, appealing color, and are heaviest for their size. Eating apples helps with bone protection and asthma, lowers cholesterol, improves the prevention of Alzheimer's disease and breast, colon, and liver cancer, and helps with diabetes management, weight loss, and more. An apple a day really does keep the doctor away!

Apricots. The best apricots are soft and springy but are not overly mushy. They should emit a lovely fragrance. Apricots are a great source of Vitamin A, which helps keep the immune system in check and is beneficial to our eye health. They are also rich in fiber, good for your heart, blood, skin, and bones.

Bananas. If you are planning to eat your bananas right away or within the next day, then choose yellow ones without bruises or brown spots. If you are buying bananas to ripen later at home, then green fruits are acceptable. Bananas contain a high amount of fiber, help to moderate blood sugar levels, improve digestive health, boost weight loss, and support heart health.

Blueberries. Blueberries should be dry, firm, and a solid blue, rather than a red or green color. Make sure that the blueberries on the bottom of the carton look edible, as well. Avoid berries with any white mold growing on them. Note that overly tiny blueberries may be sour. Blueberries are high in antioxidants, help fight cancer, aid in weight loss, boost brain health, alleviate inflammation, support digestion, and promote heart health.

Cantaloupes. Try to choose cantaloupes that give off a delicious fragrance and are either cream-colored or golden. A green cantaloupe will not taste good. The fruits should be firm with no squishy areas. Cantaloupes improve vision, prevent asthma and certain cancers, boost immunity, reduce dehydration, control diabetes, treat arthritis, aid in pregnancy, and regulate blood pressure.

Cherries. Cherries that still have their stems will last the longest. The fruits themselves should be firm, plump, deep red, and shiny. Cherries are high in potassium, act as an anti-inflammatory, help lower your risk of gout, contain lot of vitamin C (as well as a good amount of fiber), and aid in weight loss.

Figs. The best figs have their stems intact and are plump, soft, and fragrant. Avoid figs that look dry or cracked. Figs prevent constipation, lower cholesterol, prevent coronary heart disease, treat colon cancer, help to control diabetes, prevent hypertension, strengthen bones, and relieve throat pain.

Grapefruits. A good grapefruit will feel heavy for its size and will be firm and springy, rather than mushy or hard. The skin should be thin and smooth. Grapefruits are high in vitamin C and fiber and help to reduce fatigue, promote sleep, eliminate constipation, and treat urinary disorders.

Grapes. Select grapes that are firm and plump, with a healthy color to them. Those with brown spots or shriveled areas should be avoided. Grapes protect the heart, power up weight loss, help with cleaning up brain-damaging plaques, improve brain power, protect your skin from cancer, fight diabetes, and support muscle recovery.

Kiwi Fruits. Choosing the best kiwi is all about texture. A kiwi that is too hard or too soft will not taste right. Pick fruits that are firm, yet slightly springy. Kiwis are a high source of vitamin C, induce sleep, are good source of fiber, and help in digestion.

Lemons and Limes. Select lemons and limes that feel heavy for their size, are fragrant, and do not appear shriveled. They are both excellent sources of vitamin C, B6, potassium, and folate. They help with colds and sore throats and assist with constipation (hot water, lemon or lime, and honey will do the trick for all those ailments).

Mangoes. Like kiwis, your best mango will be neither rock hard, nor too mushy. It will be plump, firm, and fragrant. Mangoes are rich in fiber, prevent constipation, prevent cancer, are high in vitamin C, can cure anemia (as they are high in iron), cure acne, promote brain health, manage diabetes, and delay aging.

Oranges. A good orange will be heavy for its size and have a smooth, firm texture. Eating oranges helps to prevent various types of cancer, boosts the immune system, helps reduce the incidence kidney stones, lowers cholesterol and blood pressure, prevents ulcers, and promotes radiant skin.

Peaches. Peaches should have a deep, healthy-looking red/orange/golden color rather than green, and should be firm yet springy to the touch. Avoid those that are rock hard or are too mushy. Peaches protect eye health, being high in beta-carotene, and promote healthy skin, help maintain body weight, prevent cancer, and control high cholesterol.

Pears. Pears should be chosen without bruises or discolorations. They should be slightly soft, but still somewhat firm. Pears are a great source of fiber. They contain high quantities of Vitamin C and are a good source of minerals such as copper, iron, potassium, and magnesium. Pears are used in various treatments for gout, colitis, arthritis, and chronic gallbladder disorders.

Plums. A tasty plum will be firm yet springy and have a beautiful, deep red to purple color. Plums protect your heart with lots of potassium, a mineral that helps manage high blood pressure and reduces the risk of stroke. They also keep your bowels regular with their high fiber content, lower blood sugar, boost bone health, and improve memory.

Strawberries. Select strawberries that are bright red and fragrant with shiny green leaves. Avoid berries that look yellow or green, and double check the bottom of the carton to make sure there aren't any moldy or crushed fruits down there. Along with being a powerful antioxidant, strawberries are anti-inflammatory, fight cancers, help with healthy eyes, are high in vitamin C, and are good for bone health.

Watermelons. Select a watermelon that is heavy for its size, is firm, and gives a nice hollow sound when you tap it with your fingers. Watermelon is low in calories, may lower inflammation and oxidative stress, helps with muscle soreness, prevents macular degeneration, is good for your skin and hair, and is high in vitamins A and C.

VEGETABLES

Asparagus. Try to select asparagus stalks that are brightly colored and firm. Those that are limp or faded green will not taste as good. Choosing stalks that are of equal length and thickness will help ensure a uniform cooking time. Asparagus has a lot of vitamin K, which helps with healthy bones, along with a good amount of fiber.

Avocados. Ah, the struggle to choose a good avocado! Avocados should be firm, yet not rock hard. They should also not be squishy or too soft. Choose those without dents, cracks, or overly puckered skins. Heart-healthy avocados provide twenty essential nutrients including fiber, folate, potassium, Vitamin E, B-vitamins, and folic acid.

Beets. Beets should be fresh and firm with healthy-looking stems and leaves. They are high in vitamin A, C, E, K, and the B vitamins thiamine, riboflavin, and B12. Beets are high in minerals like calcium, iron, magnesium, potassium, zinc, copper, and manganese.

Broccoli. Select broccoli stalks that are bright green, firm, and compact. Avoid choosing yellow or flowered broccoli florets. Broccoli is high in fiber and can help lower cholesterol, promote bowel health, and regulate blood sugars, and is packed with vitamins and minerals.

Cabbages. A good cabbage will be firm, heavy for its size, and compact. They are high in fiber, very rich in vitamin K, vitamin C, and essential vitamins such as vitamin B5, B6, and B1, and help fight cancer with their phytochemicals.

Carrots. Select carrots that are firm and smooth. Carrots are high in vitamin C, anti-oxidants, dietary fiber, and beta-carotene (which is one of the most powerful antioxidants).

Cauliflower. Ideally, cauliflower florets will be cream-colored, compact, and without discoloration. Try to avoid cauliflower that is yellow, brown, spotted, or flowering. They are high in fiber, contain several anti-cancer phytochemicals, and are rich in vitamins C, B5, B6, B1, and B3.

Celery. Celery stalks should be a healthy-looking green, and their leaves should be green as well. The stalks should feel firm and crisp. Avoid celery that is limp, yellow, or blemished. Celery is noted for helping with arthritis, lowering cholesterol, aiding weight loss, detoxifying the body, and for being rich in vitamin C.

Corn. The corn's silk should be slightly moist, but not wilted or slimy. The husks should be a bright green, and the corn kernels should be slightly moist and plump. Corn is good for eye health, slows down bone loss, helps in digestion and in pregnancy (thanks to its high folic acid content), is good for diabetics, eases hypertension, and lowers bad cholesterol levels.

Cucumbers. Cucumbers should be firm, green, and well-formed. Avoid any that are shriveled, yellow, or discolored in places. They contain the anti-inflammatory flavanol, which plays a role in brain health; eating them also lowers your risk of breast, uterine, ovarian, and prostate cancers, and aids in fighting inflammation.

Eggplants. Select eggplants that are heavy for their size, are smooth and shiny, and are slightly springy to the touch. Its high fiber content aids in digestion, helps with heart disease, eliminates bad cholesterol, improves bone health, and promotes weight loss.

Garlic. Garlic heads should be plump and firm, with no soft spots or green shoots. Garlic is highly nutritious, with large amounts of manganese, vitamin B6, vitamin C, selenium, and fiber.

Green Beans. Green beans stalks should be crisp and snap, not bend, in half. Avoid soggy or shriveled stalks. Green beans reduce the risk of heart disease and colon cancer and help to regulate diabetes.

Kale. Kale leaves should be a dark green with a crisp, appealing appearance. Avoid kale that is yellow or pale green. Kale helps improve blood glucose control in diabetics, lowers the risk of cancer, reduces blood pressure, and helps prevent the development of asthma.

Lettuce, Spinach, and Other Leafy Greens. Greens should be crisp, green, and fresh, rather than slimy, wilted, or shriveled. Spinach has twice as much fiber, potassium, calcium, iron, niacin, and protein as lettuce. Which isn't to say that lettuce doesn't have its own value—lettuce is an anti-inflammatory agent, helps with unbalanced blood pressure, is a great tonic for digestive system, and has properties that help fight cancer.

Onions. Select bulbs that are heavy for their size, are dry, and do not have any soft areas. Smaller to medium onions will have the best flavor and texture. Onions have great health benefits and help treat and prevent cancer, heart disorders, and diabetes. They are high in minerals, vitamin C, vitamin B6, and dietary fiber.

Peppers. Peppers should be shiny, brightly colored, and firm. Choose those that are heavy for their size and do not have any soft spots or discoloration. They are high in vitamin A, C, and folate, can control cholesterol levels, and aid in weight loss.

Potatoes. Potatoes should be smooth, firm, and free from soft spots. Avoid those that are green, those that have eyes with sprouts, and those that appear bruised. They lower blood pressure, relieve inflammation, are a good source of potassium, and have high vitamin, mineral, and fiber content.

Summer Squash. Select squash that are shiny, smooth, firm, and unblemished. They have a huge amount of vitamin A, significant amounts of vitamin C, vitamin E, vitamin B6, and many minerals, and boosts immunity.

Tomatoes. Tomatoes should be fragrant, heavy for their size, with taut, shiny skins. Avoid overly soft or overly hard tomatoes. They have shown to be effective in fighting prostate cancer, cervical cancer, cancer of the stomach and rectum, and esophageal cancer. Tomatoes also have high amounts of vitamin C, potassium, and vitamin K, which are essential for blood clotting and controlling bleeding.

UNDERSTANDING COOKING METHODS

It's important to understand that there are many cooking methods to choose from, and some are healthier than others. In some cases, heat can even destroy the nutrients in foods, which is why many health-conscious people have been choosing to eat "raw" in recent years. In other cases, such as tomatoes, spinach, and carrots, applying heat can help to release the foods' antioxidants, which are molecules that help prevent cell damage in our bodies.

Just remember that choosing cooking methods that require the least amount of oil will help you to lose the most weight. But it's also important to balance healthiness with pleasure, and be somewhat flexible in our cooking method choices. Having something fried once in a while can be a welcome treat!

Microwaving. Using a microwave can help to minimize the destruction of food nutrients and is often the quickest way to cook or reheat an item. Placing a wet paper towel over your food can help avoid the drying effect microwaves sometimes produce. Be sure to use microwave-safe containers when cooking in this fashion.

Boiling. Boiling foods can be a great way to avoid using excess oils when cooking, especially with chicken and beef. Boiling will help preserve the nutrients in carrots, broccoli, and zucchini, but unfortunately can dissolve water-soluble vitamins in other veggies.

Steaming. Steaming is an ideal way to cook veggies, fish, chicken, you name it. It allows the food to retain its own juices and flavors. All you need is a little seasoning and maybe a sprinkle of lemon or olive oil for taste. You can purchase an inexpensive vegetable steamer at any household goods store.

Poaching. Poaching is yet another great cooking method that doesn't require excess fats and oils and is a good choice if you are looking to lose weight. Poaching uses hot water to cook foods while keeping the water below boiling. It's wonderful for cooking eggs and fish.

Broiling. To broil food, you apply direct, high heat for a short period of time. This method is usually chosen for cooking tender meats. It is not as effective for cooking veggies, as it can dehydrate them.

Grilling. Grilling is an excellent option for sealing in both flavor and nutrition. Oils and fats can safely be kept to a minimum, as meats and vegetables retain their moisture and tenderness. Try to avoid over-cooking food, however, as eating charred foods can increase your risk of certain cancers.

Stir-frying. You can get by with using only a small amount of oil with this cooking method. When stir-frying, it's best to keep your meat and veggies on the smaller size, cutting peppers, carrots, and onions into thin strips. Meats can be chopped into cubes or strips, as well. Adding rice or quinoa is always a nice touch with a stir-fry.

Frying. To fry a food, place a moderate amount of oil in a pan and heat it up to a high temperature so it sizzles. This is the normal method of cooking many of our favorite comfort foods, such as pancakes, fritters, doughnuts, fried chicken, and French fries.

Unfortunately, our culture has learned to fry almost everything, and eating too much fried food is a recipe for disaster health-wise, as it can clog one's arteries, incite weight gain, and make us more sluggish. Learning how to use fried foods as a very occasional treat can be a challenge, but you may actually come to enjoy and appreciate them much more once they are a rarity rather than a staple in your diet.

Raw. Plenty of raw foods restaurants have sprung up in recent years, especially in bigger cities like New York and Los Angeles. Dining out at one can allow you to test out whether you enjoy raw food before committing to trying it at home. Eating raw foods can help boost your vitamin, mineral, and fiber intake, and keep added sugars and fats to a minimum. But raw food doesn't agree with everyone's stomach, so it's best to go slow, incorporating a few raw meals into your diet here and there to start out.

COMPONENTS OF FOOD: MACRONUTRIENTS

Proteins, carbohydrates, and fats are called macronutrients, distinguishing them from micronutrients, such as vitamins and minerals. Macronutrients are essential for growth, development, and energy. You may hear terms such as "high-protein diet," "low-fat diet," or "no-carb diet." These are simply diets that manipulate the intake amount of a particular macronutrient to achieve a desired result. In reality, our bodies require adequate amounts of all three, so a balanced approach is usually healthier and most sustainable in the long run.

Proteins

Protein, comprised of amino acid chains, is required for building new cells, as well as repairing damaged ones. A growing child will require adequate protein intake to form healthy bones, skin, hair, and muscles. Proteins can also help to maintain muscle mass, trigger healthy hormone and enzyme production, keep the immune system functioning properly, and to provide backup energy when carbohydrates have been exhausted.

Healthy sources of protein include fish, seafood, eggs, cheese, dairy products, chicken, turkey, red meats, nuts, seeds, and beans. Vegetables and soy products also contain a certain amount of protein. On average, a woman will require fifty grams of protein a day, while a man may require up to sixty grams. Bodybuilders or athletes may naturally require more protein, as they are constantly repairing muscle and tissue. Older adults require slightly more protein because as we age, we lose muscle and bone. Eating more protein can help delay this process of deterioration.

Those who tend to over-indulge on carbohydrates such as pizza, bread, cake, cookies, and pastas may benefit from temporarily increasing their protein intake to help create more balance. A diet higher in protein can help burn more fat, so for those who are overweight, this might be a good temporary approach.

However, overdoing it on protein creates its own set of problems. When the body is starved of its main fuel source, glucose, it begins to burn fat instead. This process produces ketones, an acid, and too much of this acid can be quite dangerous. Some common side effects of ketosis are headaches, foul-smelling breath, and dryness.

Carbohydrates

If you have ever attempted any kind of weight loss regimen, you are probably familiar with how carbohydrates serve as a primary focus of many diets. Some say you should eliminate them completely, while others say it's just a matter of choosing the right *kind* of carbohydrate. Other diets require you to "count" carbohydrates.

The reality is that carbohydrates have been given a bad name due to a shift in conventional thinking about weight loss, a shift that happened in the 1990s with the Atkins high-protein diet. Prior to that, most weight loss specialists focused on low-fat diets, with low-fat products sweeping the supermarket shelves. It wasn't until there was a shift and the new fad became "low-carb" that carbohydrates developed their current bad reputation.

Most of the time, when someone mentions a "bad" carbohydrate, they are referring to a simple carbohydrate, such as white sugar, syrup, soda, cake, cookies, or beer. These are processed extremely quickly by the body, which can then result in a "crash" a few hours later. Complex carbohydrates, such as apples, oatmeal, peas, quinoa, or chickpeas, are generally processed slower by the body, resulting in more sustainable energy.

The Glycemic Index is a system to determine just how quickly a carb will boost one's blood sugar. Foods that are lower on the glycemic index, such as nuts, fruits, and veggies, will provide more steady, continuous energy and help you to avoid a blood sugar "crash."

The Dietary Guidelines for Americans suggest that one should eat between 200–300 grams of carbs per day. For those attempting to lose weight, 100–150 grams per day may produce better results. But using common sense, it's best to select your carbs from whole foods rather than processed foods, as processing can drain food of its vitamins and minerals until there is very little nutrition left.

Carbohydrates found in nature, such as nuts, seeds, fruits, vegetables, and even potatoes, will always be healthier than those created in a factory, such as chips, candy, soda, or cake. However, in very small, occasional doses, junk food can be harmless. It's always important to be flexible in one's eating, as being too rigid now can lead to binge eating later. Also, remember that heavy exercise such as running or weight lifting will always require an increase in carbohydrate intake.

Ultimately, carbohydrates are an important element of any healthy diet, and they are necessary for sustainable, long-term weight loss. Carbs are broken down into glucose, which is the body's main source of energy. This energy is needed to power our brains, our nervous systems, our kidneys, and our muscles. Carbohydrates in the form of fiber are also needed to maintain intestinal health and ensure proper bowel movements.

There are three main types of carbohydrates:

Sugars. This is the simplest form of a carb. Simple sugars are contained in milk, fruits and vegetables. Sugars can be present as fructose (in fruits), sucrose (in table sugar), or lactose (found in milk products).

Starches. A starch is a complex carb made up of a string of sugar units. Vegetables, grains, beans, and peas contain complex carbohydrates.

Fiber. Fiber is a type of complex carb that occurs naturally in veggies, fruits, grains, beans, and peas.

Fats

When it comes to fats, there is a lot of information out there to digest. For a long time, it was thought that fat was the "enemy," and weight loss experts pushed low-fat and non-fat foods uniformly.

Today, we have a better understanding, and recognize that not all fats are evil. There are actually some fats that are necessary to maintain a healthy lifestyle. These include: nuts, seeds, and avocados; plant oils such as olive, safflower, and canola oils; and Omega-3 fats, including those from salmon, herring, mackerel, flax, walnuts, and soybeans. Collectively, these are known as the "good" fats; however, they should still be consumed in moderation. Only about a quarter of your total daily calories should come from fat.

Saturated fats, hydrogenated fats, and trans fats are collectively known as the "bad" fats. Saturated fats include animal fats found in meats, cheeses, cream, ice cream, butter, lard, coconut oil, palm oil, and chicken skin. Hydrogenated fats are made through a chemical process that changes liquid vegetable oils into solid fats at room temperature. Hydrogenation can also turn oils into trans fats, which are often found in snack foods like chips and French fries or in margarines and shortening products.

When we consume too many of these bad fats, we put ourselves at a higher risk for heart attack, stroke, or heart disease. Unfortunately, these bad fats are also very tasty, so it can be difficult to change one's diet. The key is to make slow, steady, sustainable changes, learning to enjoy the taste of healthier foods one day at a time. Today, many products are packaged with the label "free from trans fats" so it's easier to select the healthiest choice at the store.

Cholesterol and Triglycerides

When discussing fats, it is also important to understand the role that cholesterol and triglycerides play. Cholesterol is a fatty substance found in animal and human tissue that plays an important role in the body. Our liver naturally produces enough cholesterol for normal functioning, but we also get extra cholesterol from meats, eggs, poultry, and dairy. If we consume too much excess cholesterol, it can clog our arteries and may lead to atherosclerosis.

Triglycerides are fats that travel through the bloodstream with cholesterol. The body both makes its own triglycerides and receives them from meat and plant oil consumption. If too many triglycerides are consumed, it may increase the risk of heart disease. Getting both your cholesterol and your triglycerides levels checked by a doctor is a good self-care action, especially if you are concerned about your weight.

COMPONENTS OF FOOD: MICRONUTRIENTS AND THE IMPORTANCE OF SUPPLEMENTS

Micronutrients are vitamins and minerals and are mandatory for maintaining our health. They allow us to produce enzymes, proper hormones, and proteins, all of which are essential for our well-being. When we experience a vitamin or mineral deficiency, our health can seriously suffer. This is why so many foods are now "fortified," meaning they have vitamins and minerals built in.

Even with our foods being fortified, we may still need to take additional vitamins and minerals as supplements in the form of capsules, tablets, powders, or in energy drinks. The FDA has established daily allowances for vitamins and minerals, which are posted on the labels of supplements for your convenience. Always be sure to follow these guidelines when taking supplements, as even herbs can be dangerous in heavy doses.

Vitamins include vitamins D, A, C, K, E, and B, and each has a different purpose. Vitamins are either fat-soluble (A, D, E, and K), or water-soluble (B and C). Fat-soluble vitamins are stored in reserve in our fat tissue, while water-soluble vitamins need to be replaced on a daily basis because the body excretes them in the urine. (If you are a vegan, you will need to take B12 as a supplement, since the only other way to get it is through eating meat.)

The body requires both macro-minerals (magnesium, sulfur, sodium, chlorine, phosphorous, calcium, and potassium), and micro-minerals, also known as trace minerals (chromium, iron, iodine, selenium, manganese, zinc, copper, and molybdenum). Minerals help the cells to carry out their important functions.

If you really want to get your vitamin and mineral intake right for your body, it's best to see a nutritionist or a naturopath who can customize your supplements to your lifestyle, health issues, and anatomy. For those seeking more general guidelines, a daily multi-vitamin, along with some vitamin C, calcium, probiotics, and digestive enzymes, makes for a good starter regimen for the average person.

THE IMPORTANCE OF DRINKING ENOUGH WATER

Proper water consumption is important for the majority of our daily bodily functions. From waste removal to sweating out toxins, regulating body temperature, producing saliva, maintaining circulation, protecting the spinal cord, keeping the skin looking beautiful, reversing the signs of aging, and lubricating the joints, water is an indispensable component of being human.

Water also acts as a counterbalance to certain foods that would otherwise cause inflammation or allergies. When we eat something our bodies can't process, we tend to gain water weight, as the body instinctively seeks to neutralize the threat with moisture. Therefore, if you've overindulged in foods you know aren't good for you, the best remedy is water. Alcohol and caffeine in particular can dehydrate the body, so recovery from their effects should involve replenishing the body with fluids.

So, how much water is "enough" water? According to the Institute of Medicine, men should consume around three liters of water per day, and women should consume about 2.2 liters per day. This will obviously vary if you are exercising a great deal, are out in the sun often, or have recently gone to the spa or a hot yoga class; in these cases, you will probably need extra water on top of the daily-recommended minimum.

FOODS TO CONSUME IN MODERATION

Refined Sugar

Refined sugars, such as corn syrups and sucrose, contain an enormous amount of calories and almost zero nutrients. This is the reason they are referred to as "empty" calories. Like credit cards, they are enticing in the short run but damaging in the long run.

An excess of refined sugars can contribute to tooth decay, not to mention bad breath. It can also overload the liver, where fructose from added sugars is turned into glycogen and stored. When the liver is overrun with excess glycogen, it creates fat, and a fatty liver can cause all kinds of health problems, as you might imagine (including NAFLD, non-alcoholic fatty liver disease).

Artificial Sugars

There is a lot of controversy over artificial sweeteners, so we'll simply state a few of the reasons why they might not be ideal for you, especially if you are trying to lose weight or stay fit.

The first is that artificial sweeteners tend to be exponentially sweeter than actual sugar, which dulls your sensitivity to naturally sweet foods like fruit. Aspartame is 200 times sweeter than sugar, and Splenda is 600 times sweeter than sugar!

Artificial sweeteners also don't send the same signals to your brain that caloric foods do. When the brain registers a dense food, heavy in calories, it releases hormones that tell your body it is satiated. Artificially sweetened foods have a thinner, less substantial consistency that may not satisfy us, causing us to eat even more.

Caffeine

Caffeine is another controversial substance that some people can consume in moderation, while others are incredibly addicted to it with very negative consequences.

In individuals with hypertension, caffeine can raise blood pressure, which is very dangerous. Overconsumption of caffeine has also been linked to insomnia, incontinence, indigestion, headaches, reduced fertility, tremors, adrenal fatigue, bone loss, and inhibited collagen response in the skin, among other ailments.

Withdrawal can be intense, but ultimately easier than something like quitting smoking. If you are looking to quit caffeine, there are lots of great alternatives available, like cacao products, green tea, yerba matte, and grain beverages.

Alcohol

Alcohol is one of those substances that affects different people differently. Those with smaller bodies will have a lower tolerance for alcohol. Chronic heavy drinking can lead to liver problems, depression, weight gain, and increased risk of heart disease and certain types of mouth cancers.

The National Institute of Alcohol Abuse and Alcoholism states that men should not exceed four drinks per day, or a total of fourteen drinks per week. For women, those numbers are three drinks a day, or a total of seven drinks per week. The American Heart Association suggests men should drink a maximum of two drinks a day, and women a maximum of one.

If you find that you are drinking in excess of seven to fourteen drinks a week, it may be time to consider moderating, or even getting support from groups like Alcoholics Anonymous.

EATING PLANS

Finding a plan of eating that works for your values and your lifestyle can bring relief from the daily decision-making we have to do in the face of such an abundance of food choices. There is no shortage of popular diets to choose from, but usually what works best long-term is something moderate and sensible and not the latest fad.

Vegetarianism and Veganism

Both vegetarians and vegans avoid eating animals; however, vegans also avoid all animal products, including honey, dairy products, and gelatin.

A plant-based diet has been indicated to protect from ailments such as obesity, diabetes, cardiovascular disease, and some types of cancer. It is possible to get all your nutrition from a vegetarian diet, but vegans will need to take B12 supplements since they cannot get vitamin B12 from a purely vegetable-based diet. (B12 deficiency can lead to anemia and nervous system damage.)

Being a vegetarian or vegan today is very easy, as there are a million "taste-alike" products on the market, including vegan sausage, vegan bacon, vegan cheeses, and milks made from almonds, hemp, coconut, rice, or even hazelnuts.

Paleo

The Paleo diet is based on the idea that cavemen were healthier and leaner than us, and that we should eat as they did to stay slim and energetic. This translates into eating anything that could be hunted or gathered, such as nuts, greens, seeds, meats, fish, fruit, etc.

Cavemen naturally didn't have pasta, cookies, or candy, so on the Paleo diet one wouldn't consume those items. The cavemen also didn't eat grains or gluten, which Paleo enthusiasts argue turns directly to sugar in your body. There is no calorie counting or portion control, however, which appeals to many people who can't stand those elements of other structured diets.

Mindful Eating

The mindfulness diet has its roots in the Buddhist tradition, and involves developing your awareness to make wise food choices based on your own inner wisdom and innate sense of what is right for your body. This is great for those who binge for emotional reasons or who eat when they're stressed.

In the mindfulness diet, you are called upon to eat slowly and purposefully, without external distractions such as the phone, radio, TV, or conversations. It means learning to pick up on your body's signals that it is full or that it is hungry again and sorting through your personal triggers for overeating. You are fully engaged in experiencing the sounds, textures, smells, sights, colors, and tastes of your food. Lastly, you are called upon to express gratitude for your meal, which can provide genuine healing energy to those who struggle with guilt, anxiety, or shame around eating.

Taking the Next Step

In an effort to practice self-love around our eating habits, we can use affirmations to rewire our patterns with food. On the next page, you will find twenty affirmations for healing your relationship to your body and its optimal nutrition.

Affirmations for Nutrition

- Planning healthy meals is a joyful experience.
- I respect and honor my body with proper nutrition.
- Today, I will choose foods that support my total well-being.
- I listen to my body and respect its limits.
- I only eat when I am calm and peaceful.
- I stop eating when I am full.
- I slow down and savor every bite.
- I radiate confidence, beauty, and peace.
- I am healing at a cellular level.
- I love myself from head to toe.
- I grow stronger and healthier each day.
- I am grateful for nature's abundance.
- I give my body all the nutrients it needs.
- I am compassionate towards myself around my eating.
- I release old negative patterns of harming myself with food.
- I only eat when I am actually hungry.
- I effortlessly maintain my ideal body weight.
- I love how my body looks and feels.
- I take delight in trying new foods.
- I now release all cravings for unhealthy foods.

Chapter 5

EXERCISE

"Exercise should be regarded as a tribute to the heart."

—GENE TUNNEY

The human being is the only animal ever to wind up a couch potato. It may have to do with the invention of television, or smart phones, or video games; regardless, every other animal lives to exult in the joy of their bodies, running, stretching, playing, jumping, hopping, and leaping.

Our bodies are similarly meant for the physical pleasure that comes from moving our limbs. If we starve our bodies of this basic need for exercise, our muscles atrophy, becoming weak and flabby; our heart and lungs function poorly; our skin grows dull; our joints become stiff; we grow depressed and anxious; we may have trouble sleeping; we gain weight; the entire quality of our lives begins to suffer.

So why do we insist on avoiding exercise? Why do we shut ourselves indoors, consuming exercise substitutes such as stimulants, opting to view the world through a series of screens? What has gone wrong in our minds that we deprive ourselves of the activity so integral to human growth and development, something that prevents disease, improves stamina, gives us our best possible figure, controls our weight, and pumps us full of positive vibes?

The answer to this question will be different for each person. For some, childhood bullying will have played a significant role in discouraging the enjoyment of sports and fitness. Today, there has been significant focus on the harmful effects of bullying, and schools and parents have more awareness about the seriousness of teasing and name-calling. But just ten to twenty years ago, this was not the case. Many kids grew up being called awful names if they weren't athletic enough. They might have received the message that they shouldn't even bother to do sports if they couldn't be the best. Or worse, they may have been physically harmed by others and decided it just wasn't worth it to fight back.

I know others who simply grew up in families where everyone smoked, drank, and overate. It is hard coming from a family like this and then breaking the mold to start exercising. If you come from an environment that rewarded addiction and apathy rather than health and self-care, starting an exercise program can be quite daunting, as it is literally going against everything you know and understand from childhood.

You may have other personal reasons for not wanting to exercise. Perhaps you're afraid of how you look running, that you'll be made fun of or judged. Perhaps you feel you don't have enough time in your busy schedule, or that there's nothing physical you enjoy doing.

Whatever your reasons for avoiding exercise may be, overcoming them is an absolute must. Exercise is a non-negotiable component of a healthy life. You can exercise any way you want, from bowling to belly dancing, but getting your heart rate up and your muscles engaged transforms the experience of being alive, elevating you to a whole new level of existence. It can boost your job performance, improve your relationships, jumpstart your sex life, amplify your memory, clear your skin, trim your fat, lower your risk of disease, and upgrade your mood from "blah" to "wow!"

In life, there is the suffering that we cannot control and there is the suffering that we *do* have control over. The suffering that comes from not exercising enough is entirely avoidable. By practicing self-care through the implementation of a physical routine, we can help to provide a buffer to the stresses and "slings and arrows of outrageous fortune" that are a natural element of life. Things will go wrong as they always will, but if we're strong, fit, and centered, we can meet these challenges successfully with poise and grace.

Exercising puts you back in touch with nature, creating an actual connection from your feet to the Earth. As you breathe deeply, inhaling and exhaling, you engage with the air and the elements, becoming more present. Climbing mountains, running through a field, swimming in the ocean, going for a hike, or making a tree house are all activities that can give you a deeper appreciation for our planet and its wonders.

Most of all, exercise is a deep expression of gratitude for being alive, for our bodies and their endless miracles. To be in a healthy, capable body that is able to run, jump, play, dance, and fight is a gift beyond measure. By exercising, we connect to the enormous good that is our birthright.

HOW OFTEN SHOULD I EXERCISE?

If you are just starting out on your exercise journey, it can be very tempting to overdo it right away, get overwhelmed, and then quit and go back to a life of zero activity. There's not one of us alive who hasn't fallen victim to this self-sabotaging trap in one way or another.

Your watchword should be "easy does it." Take things slow, listen to your body, and start small. Try to take a good, long walk for fifteen minutes every day. If that's all you can do at first, that's still great! You're on the right track. Consistency is more beneficial than quantity. Exercising four hours one day, then zero hours for the rest of the week is less effective than that persistent fifteen-minute walk each day.

Eventually you can work up to doing around thirty minutes of cardio three times a week. You can alternate this with weight-bearing exercise on off days, and then add two to three sessions of stretching or yoga in per week to make sure your muscles are relaxing and healing. Remember to always stretch and warm up before *any* exercise session.

TYPES OF EXERCISE

Did you know that there are four different types of exercise, each with a different purpose? Understanding this can be key in developing a stimulating, varied exercise routine that will keep you mentally, emotionally, and physically fit.

You will need to work on building strength in your bones and muscles, toning and shaping your core, keeping your heart functioning at peak capacity, and challenging your mental concentration. To do all this, you will need **aerobic exercise**, **strength training**, **flexibility exercises,** and **balance exercises**.

Aerobic Exercise

Aerobic exercise, also known as "cardio," gets you moving and sweating as fresh oxygen travels through your body. It is stimulating to the breath and the heart rate, and includes running, swimming, hiking, dancing and kickboxing, just to name a few common sports you might enjoy.

The Mayo Clinic suggests getting 75–150 minutes of aerobic activity per week, or at least thirty minutes of sustained physical activity such as brisk walking (or lawn mowing) per day.

What you might not know about aerobic exercise is that it has a positive effect on brain chemistry, boosting your serotonin and helping to achieve mental and emotional well-being. It can also help reduce the risk of cancer, diabetes, osteoporosis, heart disease, and depression.

Anaerobic Exercise

Anaerobic means "without oxygen" and describes exercise that is performed at a high level of intensity for a short duration. Under these circumstances, the body's demand for oxygen will be greater than the oxygen supply, so the body will turn inwards to the muscles for its energy. Some examples include sprinting, jumping rope, or racing a bike. Anaerobic exercise is great for increasing muscle strength, improving stamina, and maintaining a lean physique.

A good way to incorporate anaerobic exercise into your workout is to do interval training, such as increasing your speed for sixty seconds during a run or a swim. This shouldn't be attempted by beginners, but rather is something to work up to as an intermediate to advanced exerciser. (Remember that anaerobic exercise is not recommended for those that are pregnant.)

Weight-Bearing Exercise

Weight-bearing exercise is imperative for both the muscles and the bones. Just like your muscles, the bones are made up of living tissue, and they need to exercise in order to grow strong and sustain you into your senior years so that you can stay fit and independent.

Putting calculated stress onto the bones helps to stimulate calcium uptake, which aids in bone growth. Higher bone density is key in preventing osteoporosis. Osteoporosis is a serious threat, as around eight million women and two million men suffer from it in the United States.

Bones are also best protected from injury by healthy muscles, coordination, and balance. Studies show that six out of ten people that suffer from a hip injury, for instance, never regain their former independence, causing them to depend on others for simple tasks. By exercising regularly, *all* of this is avoidable.

Most fitness authorities recommend thirty to forty-five minutes of weight-bearing exercise about three times a week.

Exercising in the Water

Because working out in the water has little to no impact on the joints, it can be an excellent source of exercise for those with injuries, older adults suffering from osteoporosis or arthritis, and those with sensitive joints in general.

Working out in the water can be just as effective as working out on land in terms of achieving cardiovascular benefits, strength, and fat-burning. It's also a great way to switch things up if you are feeling bored by your regular workout routine.

Training in the water is like surrounding yourself with body weights: the water acts as its own form of resistance. In addition, because the effects of gravity are lessened in water, you gain greater flexibility of motion. Your lungs work harder under the strain of the water's pressure, as well.

For those that are obese or seriously overweight, exercising in the water can mean the difference between a pleasurable, rewarding work-out, and one that is fraught with stress, chafing, and frustration. Water exercise reduces pressure on the back, spine, and the knees, while cooling you off so you don't get overheated like you would outdoors. Simple jumping jacks or shuffling side to side in a shallow pool can make a wonderful start to a fulfilling, manageable exercise routine. What's more, you remain well-hidden underwater, so there's less embarrassment over fitting into tight exercise clothes.

Specialists suggest exercising in the water for around thirty minutes three times a week to lose weight.

Stretching

If you are in your younger years, you may tend to overlook stretching, considering it the "boring" part of working out. You stay limber and flexible without even trying. As we age, however, this magical power dwindles away and we start to feel sore, get cramps, and experience pain if we skimp on stretching.

Maintaining one's flexibility over one's lifetime is crucial, as the body you build now will sustain you into your golden years and will decide your future quality of life. (We have all shuddered to see an older person whose back is severely bent, forcing them to use a walker to get around.)

Warming up the calves, hamstrings, hips, quads, glutes, shoulders, neck, arms, and lower back is mandatory for avoiding injury and keeping a slender, lean profile.

Yoga

Yoga is a multifaceted form of exercise that improves posture, circulation, balance, strength, flexibility, and breath awareness, while also increasing concentration, inner peacefulness, immunity, and joy in one's body. Its physical, mental, emotional, and spiritual benefits can't be denied.

There are many different schools of yoga, and many different levels, but all involve the practice and performance of simple postures called asanas that promote health and overall well-being.

Yoga can be especially beneficial for those with injuries, as it is gentle, with each person being able to go at their own pace and perform variations if necessary. Yoga can actually help lessen back pain, arthritis, obesity, headaches, insomnia, high blood pressure, and carpal tunnel syndrome, among many other ailments.

Yoga also helps us to establish a mind-body connection that we might not get with other forms of exercise. We sink deeper into our bodies, feeling more present in the moment. This experience then gradually carries over to other parts of our lives.

Beginners should start with one hour of yoga a week and work up to two to three hours per week.

Martial Arts

Not everyone will gravitate towards martial arts, but I list them here because learning to practice a martial art can do wonders for your self-esteem and self-confidence. It can also be a healthy outlet for releasing anger and frustration and can help you develop self-defense skills that can make you feel safer in an unpredictable world.

There are a multitude of different martial art forms, and choosing the right one for you can be a fun process of exploration. You can almost always find places where you can take an introductory first class to see if you like it. Some of the most popular martial arts including American boxing, Muay Thai kickboxing, kung fu, Brazilian jiu-jitsu, krav maga (developed by the Israeli Defense Force), tae kwon do, MMA (mixed martial arts), sumo wrestling, karate, aikido capoeira, tang soo do, sambo, and judo.

Tai Chi

While technically a non-competitive martial art that originated in Taoist and Buddhist monasteries, most people practice tai chi for its incredible health benefits. It incorporates gentle stretching and movements that increase concentration and mindfulness, as well as balance, control, and flexibility.

For older adults, tai chi can help to reduce the risk of falling and getting injured. Tai chi has also been cited as a medium of healing for those suffering from Parkinson's disease.

PERSONAL TRAINERS

If you are having trouble finding an exercise routine you like, are new to exercising, or just feel stuck in a rut physically, choosing to work with a professional fitness expert can be one of the best decisions of your life. Just as we go see a therapist when we experience emotional troubles, we can go to a personal trainer for motivation, information, support, and cheerleading. This can be especially helpful if you have a "block" against exercising, or some emotional baggage around getting physical. A personal trainer can also help you to achieve your weight loss goals.

Personal trainers will work with you to create a customized exercise regimen that addresses your weaknesses and capitalizes on your strengths. They can also design workouts that accommodate injuries or handicaps. With a trainer, you will get better results faster, reduce your chances of injuring yourself, establish excellent training habits, and achieve goals that you might have found impossible alone.

Selecting the right fitness trainer for you can be a little like choosing a therapist. It's best to shop around, meet several different people, and ask them the important questions that will help you get a better idea of their approach and personality. Not everyone responds to "tough love," for example; some of us need a gentler approach, especially if we've ever been the victim of bullying or abuse.

Anyone you hire to assist you with training should have the proper credentials. They should be certified, meaning that they have passed an exam by an accredited organization such as the ACE (American Council on Exercise), the NSCA (National Strength and Conditioning Association), or the NASM (National Academy of Sports Medicine). This ensures that the person is professional, has the proper training, and is operating within a standard set of guidelines for their field.

Your personal trainer should also share some of your philosophy towards life. Do they love nature, or are they more interested in working out in the gym? Do they incorporate yoga, mindfulness, and tai chi into the workouts? Are they competitive and driven, or gentle and serene? Finding someone that you feel a solid connection with can be integral to getting the results you crave.

THE BENEFITS OF BODYWORK

It would be impossible to write about exercise without mentioning one of its greatest aspects—getting a good massage!

Massage is simply one of life's sweetest pleasures, and a wonderful way to practice self-appreciation when embarking on a new exercise regimen. Massage involves manipulating the muscles, pressing, rubbing, and relaxing the skin, the tendons and ligaments, and releasing the body's pent up tension. There are massage techniques just for the head, just for the feet, and for everything in between. Besides soothing the body after exercise, massage is beneficial for insomnia, digestive disorders, anxiety disorders, headaches, and circulation problems.

Lastly, massage can produce deep feelings of connection with others, which we all need. We can experience caring and comfort from non-sexual, therapeutic touch that can be hard to come by in our regular lives.

There are a number of different massage methods, just as there are many forms of exercise. Treat yourself and find the one that works best for you!

Swedish massage involves the use of long, kneading-like strokes and circular motions to energize and relax you.

Deep tissue massage uses more force than Swedish, getting to the deepest layers of muscle and connective tissue. This is especially helpful for those with injuries.

Sports massage is specifically geared towards people involved in a particular sport, such as tennis, running, weight lifting, or swimming, and can be used to either treat existing injuries or help avoid them.

Hot stone massage uses small, heated stones placed at various points on the body to relax and loosen your muscles. (Hot stone massage is not recommended for those with hypertension, diabetes, heart disease, or varicose veins. Check with your doctor to determine if hot stone massage is safe for you.

Shiatsu massage comes from Japan and uses localized pressure in a rhythmic sequence to loosen up knots, increase energetic flow, and produce a sense of ease and well-being. The therapist will hold each point for up to eight seconds. As no oil or lotion is used, Shiatsu is normally performed over your clothing.

Thai massage is best described as a blend of stretching and assisted yoga, as the therapist manipulates your body into different challenging poses on the floor. You remain fully clothed during Thai massage. This form of bodywork can be excellent for back pain as well as problems with balance.

Hawaiian massage, also called Lomilomi, is an aspect of traditional native Hawaiian medicine that has been passed down throughout the generations. Lomilomi incorporates the philosophy of "aloha," or love, harmony, and positive intention. It is sometimes referred to as "loving touch." It is performed in flowing, circular movements that begin at the shoulders and cascade down to the feet, almost like the practitioner is doing a dance. Lomilomi is both gentle and invigorating at the same time.

Reflexology is body work ... for your feet! Your therapist will use their fingers and hands to rub, knead, and relax your feet by apply pressure to your "reflex points" where energy is said to connect to the organs of the body. In this way, it is said that reflexology can heal the nervous system, increase endorphins, boost immunity, and relieve discomfort.

Cranial sacral massage addresses the bones in the head, the spine, and the sacrum. It also includes scalp massage, which is quite literally the most relaxing form of massage known to humankind! Cranial sacral is known to help relieve headaches, neck and back pain, and jaw pain and improve one's quality of sleep.

THE SOCIAL ASPECT OF EXERCISE

In our modern culture, it is quite easy to become isolated and lonely. More and more of us are working at home, commuting less, and doing more business online. It almost seems like we can earn a living, buy groceries, watch movies, and date all online without ever encountering a living soul!

This is surely not how humans are meant to live. That's why, in addition to exercise's many physical benefits, one cannot overlook the social joys that sports and recreation bring. One of the great pleasures of being a little kid was participating in things like Little League, playing on a dodgeball team, taking ballet classes, or going sledding in the snow with your friends.

But as we grow older and become adults, we sometimes stop doing these enjoyable social activities, getting bogged down with work and family obligations. When did we lose our love of nature? When did the magic get drained away from moving our bodies? At what point did we stop trusting other people and opening our hearts to them through shared activity?

Exercising is a great chance to meet new people. You might even meet a potential dating partner by joining a local soccer team, joining the YMCA, or taking Latin dance lessons. For almost any activity you're interested in, there is a way to incorporate the company of others.

For runners, have you ever done a half marathon? There is nothing more thrilling than running through the city with over 3000 of your fellow urbanites. In certain African cultures, everyone dances together as a social ritual. When is the last time you went out dancing? Don't be afraid to look stupid, just get out there and be among people doing something fun. Almost every night of the week, there is a way to go out and get moving. Exercise *can* be fun. It's not all a chore!

Taking the Next Step

It may seem counterintuitive to work on exercising through affirmations, but our actions originate in our minds, so if we can first establish healthy thinking around moving our bodies, the rest will follow. The next page features twenty affirmations to help you get the positive juices flowing, mentally and physically!

Affirmations for Exercise

- Today, I will allow myself to be strong and healthy.
- I care for my body and give myself the exercise I need.
- I am learning to find pleasure in exercise.
- I take the time to find physical activities I genuinely enjoy.
- Today I will give myself and others a break.
- I accept myself AS IS.
- I enjoy being in my body.
- I am open to new experiences and sensations.
- I love feeling energized and alive.
- I have the strength to defend myself.
- Today, I will treat myself to a wonderful relaxing massage.
- I love being in great shape.
- I deserve to love the body I have.
- I have deep gratitude for the pleasure of my breath.
- I breathe in hope and I breathe out joy.
- I am transforming into a healthy, fit individual.
- I compete against myself to be the best version of me.
- I release the need to compare myself to others.
- Today, I choose to be happy, productive, and positive.
- I release the need to be perfect and focus on my strengths.

Chapter 6

SLEEP

"Sleep is the golden chain that binds health and our bodies together."

—Thomas Dekker

"Sleep is the best meditation."

—Dalai Lama

Have you ever stopped to consider why sleep deprivation is used by political parties as a form of torture and as an interrogation technique? Or why it is also used as a form of indoctrination in cults to establish mind control and brainwashing?

Sleep is so precious and integral to our health that to go without it devastates us physically, psychologically, emotionally, and even spiritually. Even going through the day missing a few hours' sleep can cause your moods to fluctuate, your metabolism to go haywire, and your concentration to wane. Racking up a sleep debt by chronically getting less rest than you need can cause performance problems at work, troubles in your relationships, memory issues, a greater risk of injury and accidents, weight fluctuation, and poor decision-making.

To compound matters, our society has devoted its resources to creating shortcuts to avoid sleeping a full seven to eight hours a night. These include a laundry list of caffeine and energy drinks, stimulants that are meant to give you a "boost" so you can remain productive and sleep less. We are constantly bombarded by flashing lights, electronic signals, urban noises, and alarm clocks, all of which interrupt the natural circadian rhythms of our sleep cycle.

THE IMPORTANCE OF SLEEP

If you are trying to lose weight or maintain a recent weight loss, there is nothing quite as important as getting a good night's sleep. Sleep deprivation is currently considered among the greatest risk factors for obesity, both in children and in adults. Resting well gives you the energy you need to pursue a healthy exercise routine, and it also helps to keep your appetite hormones (ghrelin and leptin) balanced.

In terms of mental health, studies have linked sleeping poorly to depression, and as many as ninety percent of depression sufferers complain about having bad sleep habits. The bottom line is that before addressing mental disorders, it's a good idea to find out whether simply sleeping properly improves your mood and outlook on life. It may be that you need treatment for your insomnia or sleep apnea, rather than for depression.

Sleeping poorly can also damage our relationships with others. When we're tired all the time, it makes us irritated, frustrated, and annoyed. We lash out at others, or have trouble focusing on a meaningful conversation, thinning the fabric of intimacy that binds us to our loved ones. When we're chronically sleep-deprived, we may lose interest altogether in socializing, preferring to play games on our phones or browse the internet, doing anything that requires minimal effort or interaction with others.

Lastly, getting a good night's sleep is the best thing you can do to fortify your immune system against disease and illness. Proper sleep is non-negotiable if you want your immune responses to be robust and timely. If you find yourself getting colds, sore throats, or the like often, consider whether you are sleeping at least seven to eight hours a night.

If you're already sick, consider using the "rest" cure, which means simply sleeping around the clock until you feel better. This is a remarkable form of medicine that is absolutely free and can work wonders for your health. It is essentially giving your immune system the chance to repair and heal your cold from the inside out.

HOW MUCH SLEEP DO WE NEED?

The amount of sleep a person requires will vary between individuals and from life stage to life stage.

The Sleep Foundation makes the following recommendations:

- Newborns from 0–3 months old should sleep from 14–17 hours a day.

- Infants from 4–11 months old should sleep 12–15 hours a day.

- Toddlers from 1–2 years old should sleep from 11–14 hours a day.

- Preschoolers ages 3–5 should sleep 10–13 hours a day.

- School-aged children from 6–13 should sleep 9–11 hours a day.

- Teenagers 14–17 should sleep 8–10 hours a day.

- Young adults 18–25 should sleep 7–9 hours a day.

- Adults 26–64 should also sleep 7–9 hours a day.

- Older adults (over 65) should generally get 7–8 hours of sleep per day.

If you're like me, you probably didn't grow up getting all the sleep you needed and entered adulthood with a deficit already in place. I was regularly told as a teenager that I was "lazy" if I slept ten hours. These early deficits are all the more reason why you need to get proper rest as an adult, if not extra rest.

TYPES OF SLEEP

There are two main types of sleep: rapid eye movement (REM) sleep, and non-rapid eye movement (NREM) sleep. NREM is often called quiet sleep, and REM is called active sleep. Each stage of sleep fulfills a physiological and neurological purpose, and if this purpose is not executed properly, a person will feel groggy and exhausted.

NREM Sleep

Non-REM sleep has three stages. Stage 1 is the period between wakefulness and sleep, when we are quite drowsy and are just drifting off. Brain wave activity and heart rate are both slowing down. It is rare to dream during this stage of sleep. Stage 1 typically lasts about ten minutes and accounts for about five percent of total sleep time.

Stage 2 accounts for forty-five to fifty percent of total sleep time; sleepers will spend the most time in this stage throughout the night. Muscle activity is decreased and consciousness fades completely. No sounds or conversations can be heard.

Stage 3 is called slow-wave sleep (SWS). This is a very deep period where the sleeper will be highly unresponsive to outside stimuli. Tissue repair and regrowth happens during this stage, as growth hormones are released. Stage 3 accounts for about fifteen to twenty percent of sleep time. This is the sleep you're talking about when you tell others you had an especially "deep" sleep, one that was incredibly restorative. Dreaming will occur most commonly during Stage 3 sleep. If a person is prone to sleep-walking or sleep-talking, these will also happen during this stage.

REM Sleep

A baby will spend about eighty percent of their sleep time in the REM phase, a percentage which slowly decreases with age. As adults, we will spend about twenty to twenty-five percent of our sleep time in REM sleep. REM sleep happens in cycles of 90–120 minutes and is more common in the later hours before we wake up.

The dreams that are most memorable and vivid often occur during REM sleep, as the eye movements are said to be tied to our internal visualization of dream images. Accompanying the rapid eye movement is a complete muscular atonia or cessation, which is possibly in place to prevent us from acting out our dreams physically.

Research shows that REM sleep is a necessity for early childhood development and learning complex tasks. Science has noted that a longer period of time is spent in REM sleep as adults following periods of learning new tasks and taking in a lot of new information. This is referred to in sleep language as "memory consolidation."

Sleep Disorders

All of us struggle from time to time with getting a good night's rest, but when a person is chronically unable to sleep properly and it starts to seriously interfere with their job performance and relationships, it may be time to see a professional and get diagnosed for sleep disorders. There are a variety of methods used to help heal from a sleep disorder, from pharmaceuticals to hypnosis, but figuring out where the problem originates is a great first step.

Medical professionals typically use what's called a hypnogram to get a picture of your sleep cycle so they can diagnose any sleep disorders. Polysomnography measures body functions that include brain waves, eye movement, muscle activity, respiration, and heart rhythm. A graph is then created that can be used to help pinpoint where your sleep troubles are arising.

Insomnia. Insomnia describes the problem of not being able to fall asleep, waking up too early, or not being able to stay asleep for long. Insomnia affects about thirty to thirty-five percent of the population, and can last up to three months on average. Insomnia is linked to depression, stress, problems with work, and problems with relationships. It can seriously lower one's quality of life.

Short sleeper. Short sleepers are those rare folks that can function normally on less than seven hours of sleep a night. These people differ from those suffering from "insufficient sleep syndrome," who will need to catch up with naps. Natural short sleepers will not need naps and will feel great with no complaints even on four or five hours of sleep. Short sleeping has been traced to a gene mutation. While these people are lucky, they are also rare. Most of us cannot afford to skimp on sleep without facing dire consequences!

Hypersomnia. On the other side of the spectrum is the person who over-sleeps. The most common form of hypersomnia is **narcolepsy**. This disorder occurs when a person feels overwhelmingly tired. They may even fall asleep in the middle of doing a normal task. Narcolepsy can be quite dangerous if the person happens to be driving, walking, or eating at the time of their sleep attack.

Narcolepsy occurs in about 1 in 2000 people and may run in families, although not always. The latest research proposes that people with narcolepsy suffer from low levels of the neurotransmitter hypocretin, the chemical regulating arousal, appetite, and wakefulness. It is not necessary to assume you have narcolepsy just because you are uncommonly drowsy during the day. This condition should be strictly diagnosed by a medical professional.

Other types of hypersomnia disorders include **idiopathic hypersomnia**, in which a person will need to sleep twelve to fourteen hours a day; and **Kleine-Levin Syndrome**, where a person will experience intermittent episodes of excessive sleepiness.

Long sleeper. In contrast to a short sleeper, we have the long sleeper, who will simply require more sleep than the average member of the family, somewhere in the ten to twelve hours a day range. This person will sleep well with no complaints, just for longer periods than is considered normal.

It usually begins in childhood and continues throughout the person's lifetime. A long sleeper will not benefit from stimulants or drugs prescribed to keep them awake. They truly need all their sleep or they risk a host of problems at work and in relationships.

Sleep breathing disorders. It sometimes happens that what keeps a person from getting a good night's rest is not their minds, but their breathing. The most common disorders of this group are **sleep apnea** and **snoring**.

During sleep apnea, obstructions in the airway can cause you to stop breathing. When the body registers this deprivation of oxygen, it naturally wakes up, disrupting your sleep cycle. This may happen just one or two times a night, or in the worst cases, it may happen continuously. The sleeper wakes up feeling exhausted and drained. Long-term negative effects of sleep apnea and oxygen loss can include depression and higher risk for heart disease, stroke, diabetes, and hypertension. Healing from sleep apnea can sometimes require surgery to clear the nose of obstructions.

Snoring is very common, with about half the population having suffered from it at one point in their lives. It can happen at any time of the night and may be eased by switching from sleeping on one's back to sleeping on one's stomach or side. Snoring is common in those with seasonal allergies or those suffering from a head cold.

Snoring is only harmful if it wakes you up and causes you to sleep poorly. Otherwise it is merely a nuisance to those around you. You will need to see a sleep doctor to determine if your snoring is an actual sleep disorder or not.

Circadian/Sleep-wake disorders. When a person does not sleep during normal sleeping hours, they may be suffering from a sleep cycle disorder that is interrupting their natural circadian sleep rhythm.

A delayed sleep-wake phase disorder (**DSP**) occurs in a person who goes to bed later than usual and sleeps later than usual. There is some sort of two to three-hour delay in their internal sleep clock. This pattern may interfere with work duties or parental obligations and is therefore undesirable. DSP may be tied to depression, so it's important to have it properly diagnosed and treated by a doctor.

During advanced sleep-wake phase disorder (**ASP**), a person's sleep clock is set a few hours earlier than normal. They might be labeled an "early bird" because of this. These folks tend to go to bed between 6 pm and 9 pm, waking up between 2 am and 5 am. This cycle can interfere with one's social life, especially when plans are made for the evening hours.

In an effort to combat their irregular sleep cycle, sufferers may end up taking stimulants to try to stay awake longer, which only makes things worse, since they still wake up early in the morning. This disorder should be properly diagnosed by a doctor to differentiate it from depression or other malaises connected with sleep.

Shift work. Shift work—work that takes place during normal sleeping hours—may cause serious problems when a conflict arises between a person's natural circadian sleeping rhythm and the need to earn a living. Your body will want to sleep during work and be awake during the day when you're finally able to sleep.

The typical shift worker ends up losing around four hours of sleep a day to this struggle and may feel exhausted around the clock. Some people can eventually adjust to the backwardness of sleeping during the day, but not everyone is so lucky. It can be useful to take melatonin supplements for shift work if there is no way to avoid it altogether.

Jet lag. Jet lag is not a permanent disorder, but it can be difficult to deal with if you travel through different time zones often. Our circadian rhythms tend to adjust slowly, and if we travel quickly in an airplane to a new time zone, our sleep clock cannot catch up right away, leaving us sleepless and exhausted. Supplementation with melatonin can be helpful to those suffering from jet lag.

Sleep movement disorders. When the body's movements make it difficult to fall or stay asleep, it is referred to as a sleep movement disorder. The most common one is called **restless legs syndrome**. This occurs when the legs feel itchy or burning and one cannot get comfortable enough to fall asleep.

While at first you might not consider restless legs syndrome serious enough to seek medical help, over time, it can be quite detrimental to one's quality of life in terms of lost rest and anxiety. A doctor can treat your symptoms through medication as well as lifestyle changes.

One of the more troublesome sleep movement disorders is **bruxism**, or the grinding and clenching of one's teeth at night. While the jaw does naturally contract during sleep, with bruxism, the contractions are severe enough to wear down the teeth over time, unconsciously. This condition should be diagnosed and treated by a medical professional for best results.

Parasomnia. Parasomnia is the most dreaded type of sleep disorder, involving abnormal behaviors, movements, emotions, dreams, or hallucinations. All these take place during complete unconsciousness, and it can be extremely unnerving to discover you suffer from a parasomnia if you didn't know it before. You may even be putting yourself in potentially dangerous, disastrous situations, especially if you sleepwalk. Parasomnia can significantly disturb the quality of your sleep, so this condition should be treated by a medical professional and not handled alone.

Those suffering from **confusional arousal** are deeply confused upon waking, with slower speech patterns, poor memory, and occasional rage or hostility towards others. This disorder is sometimes called **sleep drunkenness**.

Sleepwalking. Also called **somnambulism**, sleepwalking happens when a person gets out of bed and begins to ambulate in their sleep, sometimes talking and reacting to dreamt events no one else can see or hear.

Sleepwalking can be very dangerous, especially in younger people or in those who walk or run far distances. A sleep specialist will need to be consulted and sleep research performed. Sometimes the sleepwalker is placed in a lab and videotaped to assess their movements at night.

Night terrors and nightmares. Bad dreams, particularly night terrors and nightmares, can be especially frightening and cause a person to sacrifice much-needed rest. These are common in reaction to traumatic events, PTSD, or injuries, but if they continue chronically, it's important to seek professional help.

People with night terrors will bolt out of their sleep screaming and sweating or kicking and thrashing, sometimes inadvertently injuring themselves or others. They will be absolutely terrified, as though they have seen a ghost. It can be very difficult, and at times dangerous, to wake a person who is going through a night terror. Chronic night terrors can damage relationships, as many people who have them feel embarrassed by their outbursts.

Bedwetting. Bedwetting occurs when a child or adult urinates in their sleep. In small children, this is somewhat natural, as the bladder muscles are just learning to contract. Most children will be able to control their bladders while sleeping by the age of five.

After the age of five, wetting the bed can be considered a sleeping disorder. Bedwetting may be induced by a shortage of the hormone vasopressin, which is excreted by the pituitary gland to reduce the amount of urine produced by the kidneys at night. Chronic bedwetting will require medical attention and treatment.

WHAT CAN BE DONE TO IMPROVE MY SLEEP?

There are many routes to take when battling one's sleeping problems. The first action might be to get diagnosed by a medical professional to ensure that there isn't a more serious medical issue underlying your sleeping issues, such as hormonal imbalance, nasal obstruction, or a mental illness. Proper diagnosis can save you from investing in prescription medications that may have negative side effects and may not even help.

If your sleeping problems are occasional, taking a sleeping pill once in a while may be harmless. But with chronic sleeping issues, dependency on medications can become a serious issue. It's always best to try the least invasive methods of healing first before pursuing chemical means. The Mayo Clinic suggests the following tips for a better night's sleep:

- Stick to a sleep schedule by setting aside at least seven to eight hours a night for rest and going to bed at the same time every night. The body will get into the habit of expecting to fall asleep at a certain hour, and this consistency will improve the quality of your rest.

- Be mindful of what you eat and drink before bed. This can help eliminate certain sleeping problems, such as digestive pain keeping you up or caffeine-induced insomnia. Even though alcohol might make you drowsy initially, it can disturb your sleep later in the night.

- Create the ideal sleeping environment by keeping your bedroom cool, quiet, and dark. Turn off screens and devices, draw the shades, and turn off anything that might make noise during the night. Put your phone on vibrate. Invest in a comfortable bed, pillow, and sheets that are soothing and make you feel relaxed.

- Perform soothing rituals such as drinking a hot cup of chamomile tea, listening to classical music, taking a hot bath, or meditating.

- Avoid napping during the day, as this can keep you from sleeping all the way through the night. Of course, if you are in a sleep deficit from the night before, then a nap may be necessary to catch up. Regardless, limit naps to thirty minutes.

- Get enough exercise. This cannot be overstated; the body needs to stretch its muscles and produce endorphins so that it can sleep properly in the nighttime. Exercising and sleeping well go hand in hand, so this should be the first area to adjust if you are experiencing insomnia. Getting enough fresh air and sunlight each day also promotes restful sleep.

- Dealing with emotional baggage from the day is important, as too many worries can easily keep you awake at night. A good exercise might be to write down all your worries in a notebook and set it aside, knowing you can come back to it in the morning. If you find you are consistently unable to wind down from the day due to uncontrollable emotions, it may be time to seek out therapy or work with a life coach.

Herbal Remedies for Falling Asleep

Herbal remedies have fewer side effects than standard sleep pharmaceuticals, so they should be tried first if you are suffering from insomnia.

These herbs promote relaxation, healing, peace of mind, and overall well-being.

Valerian. Valerian is a calming agent that comes in capsule form or in drops that can be mixed with water. Valerian will be effective for a few weeks, after which you should switch it up with a different herb before going back to valerian.

Passionflower. This herb can help ease the mind of its worries and lower stress responses. It is a mild sedative that can be combined well with other herbs. It is taken as a tincture, drops mixed with water.

California poppy. This plant is potent medicine not only for sleeping ills but for toothaches, headaches, and body aches as well. It is safe for both children and adults. It is taken as drops in water.

Herbal Remedies for Early Morning Insomnia
Some of us find it rather easy to fall asleep at night but may find we wake up too early. This can be due to a spike in our stress hormones. The following herbs can be beneficial in treating this form of morning insomnia.

Ashwagandha. This herb is common in Ayurvedic medicine and is used regularly in India to help regulate sleep. It relieves the stress that may be causing our morning insomnia when taken throughout the day in capsule or tincture form.

Magnolia bark. This staple of Chinese medicine can help regulate cortisol levels and relax the mind and body. It is also known to ease the symptoms of menopause in women. This herb is taken before bedtime and may help you to sleep a full seven to eight hours.

Lavender. Lavender can be consumed as a tea, which is calming and relaxing before bedtime and may help you to sleep longer. Spraying your pillow or sheets with lavender mist or soaking in a bath with lavender essential oils can also be quite useful in promoting healthy sleep.

Chamomile. Chamomile is nature's gentle sleep aid. It makes us drowsy and calm with no side effects, and can be used as a tea, a capsule, or a topical cream.

Using Meditation and Visualization to Fall Asleep

If you suffer from tension and anxiety that keeps you awake at night, preparing for bed with a guided meditation or visualization exercise can be especially useful in getting the mind to relax. It can be as simple as visualizing a calming atmosphere such as the beach or the forest, or you can listen to a more involved exercise recited by a voice on tape or on YouTube.

Here are a pair of visualization exercises to try before bed. You may want to record yourself reading them aloud and listen back at bedtime, or you may want to just memorize them. You can try them both and see which one is the most effective for you. Sleep well, and sweet dreams to all!

1. **The River of Sleep.** Recall, as best you can, the experience of easily falling asleep. It has happened to you countless times, and now you easily recall these memories, noticing how effortlessly you drifted off.

   See the path from wakefulness to sleep as a river. See yourself being carried along this current like a small leaf, with no power to resist the river's flow. Know that you are inevitably on your way towards sleep, and there is nothing you can do to resist.

   Surrender to the direction the river is pulling you—towards falling asleep. Feel the gentleness of the water beneath you as you drift ever closer to unconsciousness. Surrender now to a deep, deep sleep. Let the waters of sleep wash over you.

2. **Unwinding the Yarn.** Picture before you a ball of colorful yarn. This ball of yarn is wound very tight, which represents the tension in your mind and body that is keeping you awake.

Now discover the tip of the yarn and slowly begin to unwind the ball. Watch as it rolls away from you, slowing unfurling, with the string growing longer and longer. Feel and sense yourself decompressing from life's woes and worries.

Taking the Next Step

Using affirmations to achieve better sleep can actually be as effective in certain cases as medicating yourself, provided you stick with them consistently. The following page features twenty affirmations to help you unwind and focus on better self-care around resting your body.

Affirmations for Sleep

- I choose to give my body the sleep it needs.
- I give myself permission to take naps throughout the day.
- I release the need to push myself past my limits.
- I spend time every day relaxing and resting.
- I set healthy boundaries with others around my time.
- I wake up each day feeling refreshed and energized.
- When I'm sick, I stay in bed and rest.
- I get enough exercise so that I am tired at night.
- I now release all the stress and tension in my body.
- I wake up each day in a state of gratitude.
- I forgive myself for any mistakes and release the day.
- I give myself permission to stop worrying and relax.
- Today I did my best, and that is ENOUGH.
- I am enough, I do enough, I have enough.
- I embrace my sweetest dreams.
- Today I choose to be peaceful.
- I feel myself vibrating in harmony with the entire Universe.
- My bedroom is cozy, safe, and inviting.
- I feel relaxed and sleepy at the end of each day.
- I give thanks for my day and all the joy that it provided.

Chapter 7

COMMUNICATION

"We have two ears and one mouth so that we can listen twice as much as we speak."

—EPICTETUS

Effective communication is one of the chief differences between animals and humans and is what sets us apart as unique on planet Earth. Humans are the only creatures who have found a way to form symbols and use language, thus becoming capable of deep, complex thought.

Out of language grew government, education, business and commerce, the field of medicine, and the world of art. There is not a single human endeavor that does not depend heavily on effective communication. From dating to traveling to buying a home, your success is linked closely with how well you are communicating your needs, wishes, and boundaries.

Naturally, not all of us excel at communication or at language. We can't all be great leaders, writers, or public speakers. But we *can* learn tools to help us navigate conflict and resolution, and we can improve our communication with others through persistent practice.

What makes practicing healthy communication even more difficult today is the number of so-called shortcuts to connecting that technology has created, such as texting, emailing, emojis, acronyms, Snapchat, Instagram, Facebook, and the million and one dating apps that are now available.

While these inventions are entertaining and even marvelous in their own way, they may be actually hindering intimacy rather than fostering it by abbreviating the ancient art of talking with one another face-to-face. There is a whole world of understanding that can only be accomplished *in person.*

UNDERSTANDING EARLY COMMUNICATION PATTERNS

How well we communicate is often based on our early experiences with expressing our needs and wants at home. If every time we were honest and spoke our minds, we experienced shaming or rage from our caregivers, then we will no doubt struggle to be direct and forthright as adults. We instead start to find more underhanded, passive-aggressive ways to get our point across, or we may simply implode, refusing to let anyone in and completely withdrawing from the world of healthy communication altogether.

Others may have experienced abandonment very early on in our lives, either emotionally, physically, or both. This may have led to their stopping communicating authentically and to simply agreeing with everything, going along with whatever others wanted or decided just to avoid rocking the boat. Instead of healthy communication, they begin to practice something more along the lines of perpetual acquiescence, a total surrender to others at the expense of their real desires, needs, and opinions.

There are still others who grew up in an environment where no one listened, where they simply couldn't be heard. This may have taught them that the only way to accomplish anything was to yell, rage and scream, or throw a tantrum.

These forms of communication may have got the job done in those toxic environments, but now in our lives these modes are no longer effective and may in fact be driving others away. Through our faulty methods of communicating, we are ensuring we will never receive the love, respect, and support that we crave so much underneath. Real communication carries with it the risk of conflict, and that is exactly what makes it so difficult for many of us. But mastering a few skills can make all the difference in our communication, and in the quality of our lives.

ACTIVE LISTENING

As the quote at the beginning of this chapter suggests, communication is far more than just speaking effectively. It involves a specific type of listening, one that is active rather than passive. It means engaging with your conversation partner in an open, empathetic way that ensures your connection is a collaboration rather than a contest.

Active listening involves giving feedback at regular intervals to the person speaking, such as a nod, a gesture, or a verbal affirmation to let them know you're following along. This can also be accomplished with prolonged eye contact and positive facial expressions. These encouraging responses should be kept brief so as not to draw attention away from the speaker, but most people will be grateful to receive your approval while they're talking.

If you don't understand something, it's best to stop and ask questions to clarify. The tools of summarizing, probing, reflecting, and paraphrasing what has been said work well to keep a conversation on track and make sure both parties are on the same page.

All of this can—and should—be done without interrupting the other person. When we interrupt, it means we're thinking more about what we are planning to say than what the other person is trying to communicate. Interrupting is sometimes a normal expression of enthusiasm, so if you find yourself doing it, simply acknowledge it, and allow the other person to resume.

When it's your turn to talk, it's always good to give appropriate feedback, which may mean validating the other person's emotions or story. You can say such things as, "I'm so sorry to hear that happened," or "I hear your frustration." Sometimes people aren't looking for advice, but just want to "be heard."

MINIMIZING DISTRACTIONS

Have you ever spoken with someone who had their phone out and was half-texting while you talk to them? How did it make you feel? Did you feel valued, honored, and truly encountered? Or did you feel ignored, minimized, or even insulted?

It's next to impossible to establish good communication if our devices are getting in the way. If you intend to have any sort of serious interaction with someone, it's best to unplug. Put down the phone, or else turn it off; turn off the computer; take out the earbuds and turn off the TV. Communicating isn't something we can multi-task, not if we're serious about connecting emotionally with the other party.

Making time in a relationship to talk to each other in a quiet setting without distractions is an important building block of intimacy and partnership. In our modern times, we have almost continuous pseudo-contact with everyone through social media, texting, email, and Facetime, but this isn't the same as actually sitting across from someone and experiencing them fully, in person, with all their energy, facial expressions, body movements, and, yes, even smells. As I said earlier, there is simply no substitute for face-to-face communication.

If you are entering into a business partnership with someone, why not consider meeting them in person at an office? If you're hiring someone for a task, why not sit down with them and discuss things in the flesh? This may seem old-fashioned in our world of non-stop remote technology, but it will lead to more solid foundations for any type of relationships, whether romantic, professional, or social.

NON-VERBAL COMMUNICATION

Before we even begin to speak, we are already communicating with others through our body language. We are constantly communicating and receiving communication in the form of eye contact, facial expressions, body movements, proximity, and posture. If you've ever been to see a dance performance, you can verify the tremendous power of the human body to communicate grief, joy, loss and triumph, all without a sound.

Many of us may have unconsciously developed patterns of non-verbal communication that are sabotaging our efforts to connect peacefully and lovingly with others. We store years of trauma and pain in our bodies. We may find our arms crossed, our torsos rigid, and our facial expressions harsh, all while intending to project a more welcoming vibe. Alternatively, we may be eager to connect, but find ourselves avoiding eye contact, which may be a bad habit from growing up in an authoritarian environment.

Opening our arms, creating a neutral, empathetic facial expression, and looking directly into others' eyes are all excellent ways of showing someone that you are available and approachable and ready to connect without conflict. This holds true whether you are giving a speech in front of thousands of people, making a presentation in a boardroom, or simply meeting an old friend for lunch. People will respond to your body language almost as much as they respond to the words you say, so take the time to examine your own body language and determine if it is working at cross-purposes to your personal goals.

Another important aspect of non-verbal communication is the ability to read between the lines when receiving messages from others. Sometimes someone may be saying one thing, while their body is saying another. Ignoring non-verbal messages can be devastating to forming healthy relationships. Active listening means taking in all the cues and evaluating what is really happening below the surface in any given situation.

Cultural heritage can greatly influence non-verbal communication, as well. Anyone who grew up in an Italian home, for instance, has probably experienced exaggerated hand gestures and lively banter. Conversely, those who are raised in English homes may learn to be exceedingly polite and reserved. When individuals from different backgrounds come together to communicate, it's important to remember that everyone is entering the playing field with a different set of "norms."

PHYSICAL TOUCH AS COMMUNICATION

Physical touch can be a very important aspect of communication in personal relationships. Just as babies need to be held, so, too, do adults need to feel the physical expression of love.

Hugs, kisses, and pats on the back are all the natural currency of intimacy, and when these are withheld, it thins the fabric of closeness. Everyone will have a different degree of comfort with public displays of affection, but there's no denying that human touch is an active ingredient in healthy communication between people that love one another.

Learning how to touch others appropriately in the workplace can be important for establishing safety, good boundaries, and a sense of trust. Putting your hand on someone's shoulder, offering a hug, or patting someone on the back shows humanity and warmth and makes people feel validated on a physical and emotional level.

Of course, in our current professional landscape, we are dealing with unprecedented revelations about sexual abuse and assault in the workplace. It's important to take this trend seriously and to create new protocols for nurturing safe environments. If you are in a position of authority, always ask others if it's okay to touch them. That holds true whether you are teaching yoga, recording music, or working as a personal trainer. People feel good when they're offered choices and their boundaries are respected. If they have a history of abuse, they may choose not to be touched, and this is perfectly valid and should be respected without questioning.

"ACTIONS SPEAK LOUDER THAN WORDS"

We've all heard this catchphrase, but what does it really mean in terms of communication? Well, it means that if you are saying one thing but are doing another thing, or are making promises you can't keep, you are communicating to others that you don't mean what you say, and the integrity of your words becomes polluted. People end up no longer trusting you and they stop listening to anything you say.

If a parent or spouse says they "love" you, but then treat you abusively or even violently, they are communicating a mixed message. When in doubt, our minds will weigh actions as more important than words.

Our words will mean very little if we don't back them up with matching actions. So communicating goes beyond just what you say. It also concerns exactly what message you want to send to people about your values and your beliefs.

TAILORING YOUR MESSAGE TO YOUR AUDIENCE

One important aspect of good communication is to always be aware of your audience. We meet a vast amount of people in our everyday lives, and knowing the right tone, subject matter, and vernacular to use with each person takes some discernment.

For instance, it's usually not appropriate to use internet-popularized acronyms such as "LOL" or "YOLO" in a professional setting. It's also probably not appropriate to send your lover a "memo" when trying to share your feelings with them. You wouldn't discuss politics with a child, and you probably can't get your grandparents to understand the latest technical gadget on the market.

Much of this may seem common sense, but it goes to show how each relationship in our lives requires its own unique approach when it comes to communicating. You may end up learning the hard way that some folks are only comfortable with small talk and just can't handle a deeper conversation. That's okay; we can hold different people at different emotional distances and have respect for them all.

FIGHTING FAIR

All relationships, if they are honest and reciprocal, have conflict. Conflict is simply a part of life, and if we choose to face it rather than run from it, conflict can actually bring us closer to the other party.

But there is a healthy way to handle conflict, and an unhealthy way. Yelling, screaming, shaming, raging, hitting, and bullying are all ineffectual ways of solving a crisis. All these modes of communication do is to incite more chaos and more drama. They may be comfortable and familiar, but ultimately, they are not going to accomplish what you want them to. In fact, they usually have the opposite effect.

It's normal to feel frightened during a conflict. If you can hold onto that fear and allow it to make you vulnerable, you are already taking a step in the right direction. You don't need to puff up and become invincible. If you feel scared, just *be scared*. Sometimes all it takes is for the other person to see that you're human and they will back down.

Choosing the right time and setting to have a healthy fight is important, too. It's not fair to begin an argument with your spouse just as they are going off to give an important presentation, for instance. If you're planning to discuss finances, don't do it right before bed, when everyone is tired. This only increases the chances that the conversation might go in a nasty direction. Instead, try to have conversation on important topics early in the day when everyone is well rested and well fed. Remember the acronym of HALT (Hungry, Angry, Lonely, Tired) and try not to delve into deep waters if you're feeling any of these four states.

You also shouldn't sit on your feelings and let resentments build up over time. Get in the habit of addressing issues as they arise. If your partner asks you, "What's wrong?" be honest and let him or her know how you're feeling. This can really help diffuse built-up antagonism that is the result of sitting on hurt feelings and not sharing them.

Be direct. Instead of telling your friends what your partner is doing wrong, talk to your partner directly, taking the risk to be honest. You will feel so much relief when you take this approach, rather than the indirect, passive-aggressive one.

Remember that your partner is not the same person as you and will respond differently to situations and stimuli. This person has their own thoughts and feelings, their own history of traumas, and their own defense mechanisms. Try harder to understand their point of view and put yourself in their shoes. Everyone is doing the best they can with the tools they currently possess.

When you're arguing, allow the other person their turn to say what's on their mind. If they walk out of the room, allow them to do so; don't chase them, just let them come back when they're ready. Avoid engaging in power struggles by trying to have the last word. Not all battles are worth fighting.

Keep the focus on yourself when you talk by using "I" statements. Rather than saying, "You are so sloppy and you're driving me crazy!" consider saying, "I feel out of control when things are so messy. I feel like we should work on organizing our space better." This can really have a calming effect on the other person, letting them know that you're not accusing them or shaming them, but only trying to address something that is an issue for *you*.

Lastly, if things get heated, know when to walk away. You can always come back and resume an argument later, or even the next day. There's simply no need to let things get out of control. Knowing when to stop talking and take a break is an important aspect of being a responsible and trustworthy partner. It means you value the relationship more than you value being right.

PUBLIC SPEAKING

Public speaking is such an important life skill that most colleges require it as part of their core curriculum. There are countless situations in life where you will be called upon to speak to a group of people. Understanding that this is a learnable skill can bring some relief, especially if the idea of public speaking fills you with dread and panic.

In addition to reading this section, I highly suggest taking a course at a community college or other local establishment on public speaking to get a chance to practice and hone your skills. Taking a class lets you see that there are others who struggle to be comfortable in front of an audience. It also gives you the chance to practice, over and over, getting up and making a speech in a low-key, low-stakes setting. Believe it or not, it can actually become quite enjoyable.

There are a few cardinal rules in public speaking concerning subject matter, the most important of which is to choose subject matter to match your audience. You may be incredibly interested in an obscure author who wrote upside-down, but will your audience share your enthusiasm? Instead, they might enjoy hearing about popular authors they are more familiar with. You can always throw in a reference to your obscure literary crush for a dash of color.

Types of Public Speaking

There are typically three types of public speeches: **demonstrations, persuasions**, and **informational sessions**. A demonstration will explain how to do something, an informational session will give facts and stories about a topic, and a persuasive speech will aim to convince an audience of a certain point of view, belief, or value.

Persuasive speeches are used by politicians, community activists, and even by children who want their parents to buy them something from the store. With persuasive speeches, there is a concept of "incrementalism" which will help you to win over your audience. Incrementalism means that people can only be swayed in increments towards another opinion than the one they hold.

We can see this clearly with the discussion surrounding gun control laws. If you went to make a speech in front of the NRA, for instance, advocating no more guns, no one would listen to you because there is too large of a gap between your point of view and the audience's. However, if you gave a speech advocating a small change in the licensing of guns, you may have a good chance of swaying parts of the audience towards your goal, because you are doing so incrementally.

Public speaking requires both excellent preparation and organization. The more passionately you feel about your subject matter, the more prepared you must be in terms of facts and figures so that raw feeling doesn't replace data and information.

A good rule of thumb is to practice the rule of three. Choose three main points to support every statement you want to make. Jotting these down in an outline can work wonders for helping to keep you on track during a debate or a speech.

Make eye contact with your audience and try to look at people from all parts of the audience, not just the front row. Thank them for listening and coming. Create a warm feeling of community that engages everyone in attendance. When people feel included and noticed, they will be more likely to perk up and really engage with your presentation.

Taking the Next Step

Learning to communicate better is a gradual process; it won't happen overnight. There will setbacks and steps forward, as with any new skill. Use the twenty affirmations on the next page to help you break through those old blocks that are keeping you from expressing exactly what you want and mean.

Affirmations for Communication

- Today I will listen to others and really hear them.
- Today I will listen more than I speak.
- I always look others in the eyes when I speak with them.
- I am mindful of my body language.
- I open my heart to give and receive love.
- I let others finish their sentences.
- I love sharing my thoughts and opinions with others freely.
- I find it easy to crack jokes and share my laughter.
- Communicating with other people is easy and fun.
- I use language to express what I feel.
- I always answer my phone.
- I allow others to express their opinions openly and honestly.
- I always speak from the heart.
- I own my mistakes and apologize as needed.
- I know that I don't have to be perfect.
- I express myself in a calm, confident manner.
- I am at ease in front of large groups.
- I take a genuine interest in other people.
- I am honest and straightforward with everyone I meet.
- I am sincere and forthright in my communication.

Chapter 8

TIME MANAGEMENT

"Time is really the only capital that any human being has, and the only thing he can't afford to lose."

—THOMAS EDISON

"Habitual procrastinators will readily testify to all the lost opportunities, missed deadlines, failed relation-ships and even monetary losses incurred just because of one nasty habit of putting things off until it is often too late."

—STEPHEN RICHARDS

Time, like gravity, the sun, the winds, and the sea, is a force of nature that we have no power to alter or amend. Yet human life is filled with attempts to do just this—stop time in its tracks, delay time, accelerate time, or save time. Many of us have an antagonistic relationship with the clock, always running behind, wishing we simply had another day in the week or another hour in the day. This damaged relationship with time can cause tremendous stress, leading us to pursue self-destructive coping behaviors such as drinking more and more caffeine or sleeping less.

Yet exactly how we spend our time eludes us. Somehow there's never enough time for the activities most dear to our hearts, yet we spend hours on social media or watching television shows. We misspend our time, then feel cheated and resentful. We procrastinate on important tasks, then feel like a victim of circumstance when faced with imminent deadlines.

It's tempting to believe that if we got on a better schedule, had a better time-tracking app, had an assistant, a better alarm clock, or better hours at work that these things would solve our problems with time. Sometimes this is the case, but more often than not, our problems with time are but symptoms of a much more profound dysfunction.

It may be that we hate our life's work and need to discover a whole new career that fills us with excitement and joy, work that we would be eager to show up to every day. Or it may be that we need to overhaul our health, implementing a plan of exercise, taking supplements, and learning a whole new approach to eating. In short, tackling our issues with time may require a makeover of our whole lives, not just a quick fix with an energy drink.

So often our relationship with time is a reflection of our relationship with ourselves and with others. If we're in flight, not wishing to be present and face our circumstances, we will constantly be struggling with time management. This issue will mask deeper problems, such as fear of intimacy and fear of commitment. We may say we love someone but find that when the time comes to show up for them, we're always running late. Our true feelings of resistance and ambivalence often manifest as tardiness.

Respect for our own and others' time—or lack thereof—can be a true sign of the health of our relationships. Growing up, did your family spend enough time with you? Or were you neglected, always feeling shortchanged? We may unconsciously replay patterns of time management from our childhoods.

For instance, if your father never valued his time with you, you may grow up to be someone who doesn't value their own time very much, and who doesn't make time for healthy solitude or self-care. Overcompensation for early childhood patterns with time is also common. If your mother was always late, scattered, and disorganized, you may have grown up to be an over-achiever, stuffing your day with tasks and activities, never taking a day off.

TIME TRACKING

When someone with time issues first approaches me, I begin by asking them to take a photograph of how they spend their time. This task of "time tracking" can seem daunting, but it is similar to keeping track of the money that you earn and spend. Today there are some excellent time-tracking apps you can install on your phone that will help you to discover exactly where you are "losing" time.

The results can be very surprising, to say the least. Sometimes this clarity is all it takes to jumpstart a new regimen of better time management. Sometimes it is the starting point for delving into much bigger issues, such as dealing with addictions, difficult relationships, or a career overhaul.

During this process, you will be assigning categories to your time, such as eating, sleeping, working, traveling, social media, entertainment, reading, childcare, dating, dog care, etc. Then you will begin just by observing and recording how much time is spent on these activities each day. After about thirty days, you can look at your averages and see a clear picture of what's happening.

There may be some excesses and some glaring deficiencies. Do you see balance in your time spending? Have you made time for friendship, family, and romance? Have you made time for learning new things, taking a class, or discovering a new hobby? Do you set aside time for nature, spirituality, and prayer? What about solitude and reflection? Do you get enough sleep? All these questions can be answered by looking at your time tracking results.

Eliminating Personal "Time-Wasters"

In tracking your time, you may have noticed some serious time-wasting activities such as Facebook, playing solitaire, gossiping, watching TV, or snacking. These time-zappers are lowering your quality of life and need to be dealt with. If you're not willing to stop them altogether, then creating manageable parameters for each is a good idea.

For instance, you might decide that you will spend twenty minutes on social media in the mornings and leave it alone the rest of the day. That way, you are still participating, but you're doing so in a way that doesn't inhibit your productivity or keep you from doing other stuff you love.

BLOCKING DISTRACTIONS

Recently, while I was trying to get some work done, my phone was positively exploding with beeps, bloops, blops, and buzzes. Every app seemed to have its own special noise to disturb my writing schedule which, added to the regular noises of phone calls, texts, and emails, was creating a cacophony of interruption. I found I could hardly write one sentence without being distracted. It wasn't until I finally turned my phone off that I was able to settle into my work.

Sometimes the only way to get stuff done is to block distractions. These include the phone, social media, the news, the neighbors, noise from the street, noise from pets, and noise from kids. Creating a sacred time for yourself when nothing is competing with your attention is very important, especially when taking on creative work.

In addition, we all need solitude—that healthy downtime when we can go inward and meditate on our dreams, goals, and emotions without having to instantly respond to an Instagram alert or a social text.

Today's technology is incredible, but we need to tune it out from time to time for our own sanity and renewal.

SETTING TIME LIMITS FOR TASKS

Along the same lines as limiting social media is the idea of setting time limits each day for common tasks. These might include cleaning the house, doing laundry, checking emails, shopping and cooking, and redecorating.

Instead of trying to finish any of these items in a single go, try setting a manageable time limit for each. This will bring more serenity into your life. Spend twenty minutes cleaning up, and if you don't finish, just resume the following day. Spend fifteen minutes opening emails, and what doesn't get done today, you will address tomorrow. This way, you can avoid the pitfall of losing track of time by bingeing on a single activity that mysteriously eats up your whole day against your will.

TIME PIE CHART

Once you have completed your time tracking, you may want to create a time pie chart to establish all the categories you want in your life. This can be an excellent way to start a shift into more life balance. Make sure you include time for exercise, hanging out with friends, reading, and relaxing. When life is more balanced, our time is more productive because we're not functioning out of a deficit. If your job doesn't allow you to lead a balanced life, ask yourself whether the financial payoff is really worth the deficits you are creating in terms of enjoyment, personal fulfillment, and serenity.

LEARNING TO SAY "NO"

One of the most common features of people who struggle with time management is their inability to utter the word "no." They say yes to all kinds of requests in order to be "nice," to be helpful, or to be needed, only to feel totally overwhelmed by how much is on their plates.

Often, these types are found doing tons of charity work, volunteering at their kids' school, being on the neighborhood watch team, working overtime at the office, helping friends move, and watching other people's pets. Their instincts might be in the right place of wanting to help others, but the consequences of this can be catastrophic. Sometimes it's simply necessary to tell your boss "no" in order to maintain time commitments to family, friends, and self. Sometimes it's important to just trust the Universe that everything will get done—even if not by you.

If you are the proverbial "people-pleaser" type, you may have to swing the pendulum to the opposite direction temporarily by placing a moratorium on helping others. For just thirty days, try to only concentrate on yourself. When was the last time you got a massage or went to the spa? When did you last snuggle under the covers and read a good book? Have you made time to doing something fun with a friend lately?

If you chronically over-commit your time, you may need to practice a "fast" from accepting requests from other people and just pull your energies inwards, towards self-repair. This can be difficult, but it is not impossible. If people really care about you, they will support your self-care and simply ask someone else to help them out.

People who overcommit often bear the family role of the "Hero," like we discussed in Chapter 2. They are the ones who everyone else counts on. It can be a source of ego-deflation to stop saving and helping other people. You might feel like you're losing your identity. But even heroes need downtime. You can't really be of service to others if you're tired, depleted, and miserable. That is a form of "emotional debting" to yourself.

It might be tricky to change this pattern in your life, but over time, people will come to respect you more for setting healthy boundaries and respecting your own time. They will see you as an excellent example of someone who is managing their time and will admire you for it.

WORKAHOLISM

You may hear a friend jokingly refer to themselves as a "workaholic," but workaholism is far from a joke. It is a real addiction—an addiction to constant busyness, productivity, and accomplishment.

Many companies and corporations encourage workaholism because it helps maintain their bottom lines. In this paradigm, the harder and longer you work, the more you are rewarded and respected. The workaholic mentality is built into our national consciousness. We watch shows like *Shark Tank* that celebrate hard workers with "entrepreneurial spirits" who tirelessly pursue their goals. We praise the man or woman who is "doing it all."

While these ideals have their merits, as human beings we cannot sustain a life that places work above all other pursuits. To do so is to invite eventual illness, depression, and emotional, creative, and spiritual deprivation. Work was never meant to replace relationships, fun, meditation, exercise, creative pursuits, or hobbies. It's meant to sustain us and provide income, but when this takes over our whole lives, it is no longer serving our highest good.

Recovering from workaholism may mean radically shifting your ideas about what is worth spending time on. Begin to take note of which activities you consider a "waste of time." See how much resistance you have to taking naps. Discover how much of your identity is wrapped up in what you accomplish each day.

As you slowly survey your life, you may be amazed at the degree to which workaholism dominates. Healing means striving for balance. It means doing activities that seem counterintuitive, such as napping, playing games, and sunbathing. It means slowly relinquishing the idea that your worth is based on what you do, rather than who you are. After all, you are a human being rather than a human doing, as they say!

Most workaholics grew up in a chaotic family environment, and thus feel a strong need to control their life through constant hard work and driving ambition. It can be hard to acknowledge this, as few people will be willing to say this is a bad reaction. Most people will admire the workaholic type and put them on a pedestal. But in reality, the workaholic is filled with fear—fear of the future, fear of not being good enough, fear of feeling their feelings, and fear of being in the moment. Working can become a powerful drug in supporting self-avoidance. It must be healed slowly and gently, just like any other addiction.

DEALING WITH PERFECTIONISM

Another very common characteristic of those who struggle with time management is perfectionism. A perfectionist will spend ten hours on a project that is only meant to take thirty minutes. The project will turn out amazing, but in the meantime, friends and family will have been neglected, self-care has been ignored, and even sleep has been sacrificed. This pattern is self-destructive, even though the perfectionist might feel incredible pride in the results they achieve.

Learning to just do your best and let go is an important aspect of recovering from "time debting." Not everything has to be a perfect "10;" sometimes it's okay to just do things at a level 7 and call it a day. If you are a professional and good at what you do, the reality is there is probably very little difference between your 7 and your 10, and no one will really notice the difference!

As someone who has struggled with writer's block, I eventually had to just "write badly" in order to overcome it. What I found is that when I choose to "write badly," my writing comes out pretty close to how it sounds when I'm writing "well." You will have to experiment to see how true this is in your own life, but you will be amazed by how useless your perfectionism can be sometimes in terms of improving results.

In the end, much of our perfectionism comes from fear. We're afraid we're not good enough, so we feel we have to compensate by doing an extra-special job on everything we touch. We're afraid we're not doing enough, that we're falling behind, that we're failing, so we constantly try to balance the scales by exceeding others' expectations. This can create a lifelong pattern of over-exertion, which drains us and leaves us feeling worn to the bone.

Learning to accept that we are enough—that we do enough and we have enough—is the way to overcome perfectionism. We can aim to do a good job, rather than a perfect one, surrendering the results to the Universe and trusting that we've done our best. Adopting this attitude can free up a lot more time to just have fun, enjoy the outdoors, and enjoy the people around us. Life is too short to let perfectionism rob us of our time.

LEARNING TO PRIORITIZE

For some people, prioritizing tasks does not come easy. They see everything as equally important and find it hard to assign a level of urgency to each item on their to-do list. This is the time management equivalent of those people who struggle to block out certain sounds in a crowded restaurant and just hear all noise as equally demanding on their ears.

I often suggest making a list of must-do's for the day, along with a list of nice-to-do's. Breaking your day down into what absolutely must be accomplished versus what you would like to accomplish is a good way to simplify and prioritize. Your must-do list might look like, "Show up to work. Take dog out. Eat." And your nice-to-do list might say, "Exercise. Read. Call so-and-so. Watch a movie."

Bear in mind that our energy in the morning is our "peak energy." As the day progresses, we grow less focused and less creative. It's always best to place your most important and creative tasks in the early hours when you are most alert and engaged.

LEARNING TO DELEGATE

Do you find it hard to ask others for help with important tasks? Are you self-employed, doing everything at your job on your own? Do you live alone or work alone? If you are struggling to manage your time, you may have not even stopped to consider the obvious fact that doing things alone takes more time than doing things with help from others.

You may be the self-sufficient type, someone that prides themselves on accomplishing everything on your own. This may feed your ego, but ultimately your life will be unmanageable. We as humans are social creatures and we're meant to work in partnership with other human beings.

Right now, some of your tasks are surely delegated. You hire a mechanic, hire a housekeeper, hire childcare, and hire someone to cut your hair. Imagine if you took it to the extreme and tried to do all those tasks on your own? Life would be impossible.

So next time you have extra work on your plate, why not try enlisting a co-worker's help? Hiring an intern? Try engaging others in your tasks and discover how much faster and more efficient you can be when you stop trying to be like a Hindu goddess with eight arms!

DEALING WITH PROCRASTINATION

Procrastination is defined as delaying or postponing a task that needs to get done. This can be at work, at school, at home, or socially. Procrastinating can have very negative effects on our lives, including a reduction in income, poor health, lowered immune response, diminished social lives, higher levels of anxiety and depression, and lowered self-esteem.

There are several types of procrastinators. The first type is the adrenaline junkie. Have you ever waited until the last moment before doing something that needed to be done, and felt an incredible rush from the close call? Procrastination can produce adrenaline, that fight-or-flight hormone that gives us a certain thrilling rush. For many children who grew up in chaotic, stressful households, this adrenaline rush has become normalized. Now, as grown-ups, they simply cannot function without creating some kind of crisis or last-minute emergency that they have to handle, maintaining the cycle of fight-or-flight living.

Peacefulness and being on time seem too boring, so the adrenaline junkie creates more drama by paying bills late, being late to work, and sabotaging important meetings. Stability is undesirable, as is serenity, to this type of procrastinator. For the chronic procrastinator who thrives on adrenaline, learning to embrace calm, peace, and an even emotional keel is key. It can be difficult to surrender the idea that life should be a series of roller-coaster-like thrills. The adrenaline-junkie procrastinator will have to learn to gain a rush from other less self-destructive activities, like go-carts, off-road biking, or scuba diving. Taking risks is a wonderful and exciting part of life, but when it threatens your job or personal relationships, it's time to reconsider putting things off as a means of getting a thrill.

Another type of procrastinator is the one who is terrified of making a mistake, and simply postpones the inevitable moment when they will have to give up unlimited choices for a single choice. This is basically a fear of commitment masked as avoidance.

Yet another type of procrastinator puts off their tasks because they feel inadequate and don't want to face feelings of inferiority and of being an imposter. These types of procrastinators have to face their deepest feelings of unworthiness in order to recover, and they may require the assistance of a therapist or support group.

Thankfully, there are some excellent solutions to procrastinating; it need not ruin your life. One of my favorites is implementing a reward system. If you've ever tried to motivate a child or a dog with a treat or promise of a fun activity, then you know firsthand the difference that a reward can make. If you have something particularly challenging you need to do and don't want to do it, try creating an especially enticing reward for yourself to enjoy after you complete the action. This could be getting a delicious smoothie, going to see a movie, going to the spa, or enjoying a glass of red wine. Whatever you choose, it should be something wonderful that will truly motivate you to get your task done.

Another important solution is to practice forgiveness. Until you really let go of the anger you have towards yourself for getting behind in your duties and tasks, it will probably be hard to move forward. Accept that you are human. Admit you are behind and contact anyone who is waiting for you to let them know you acknowledge your tardiness. Give yourself a break and understand that you are always doing the best you can. Feeling compassion towards yourself can liberate you to make a fresh start and let you focus on what you can do today to move forward.

Accountability is also an important component of healing from procrastination. Knowing someone else cares about seeing you succeed can create motivation and reduce the feeling of taking actions in a vacuum. If you can, start an accountability group with friends or co-workers to take advantage of positive peer pressure. For instance, if you have a goal of running a half-marathon but have been procrastinating on your training, why not start a running group with friends? This not only provides a more social aspect to a task or activity, but it helps keep you in check now that you have made a commitment to other people who are counting on you.

Taking the Next Step

If you are ready to begin working on your issues with time, then the affirmations on the next page will really help you to move forward. I have included twenty self-affirming sentences that you can print, record, or just read, customized to help those who struggle with tardiness, procrastination, or time-wasting.

Affirmations for Time Management

- I am responsible with my time and spend it wisely.
- I release the need to fill my life with time-wasters.
- I let go of unhealthy distractions.
- I arrive early to appointments.
- I set limits on my time that make life easier.
- I set healthy boundaries with others around my time.
- I always leave enough time for fun.
- I lived a balanced life, spending time with friends and family.
- I spend time dating and nourishing myself romantically.
- It is safe to say, "No."
- I effortlessly complete work, projects, and tasks on time.
- I release the need to sabotage my efforts through tardiness.
- I start and end things on time.
- I find it easy to be ahead of schedule.
- I find it easy to focus on the task at hand.
- I take vacations, short trips, and excursions often.
- I make time to have a personal life outside of work.
- I have enough time, love, and money.
- I put the most important things in life first.
- I surrender to the perfect timing of the Universe.

Chapter 9

VALUES

"Open your arms to change, but don't let go of your values."

—DALAI LAMA

"If you don't stick to your values when they're being tested, they're not values; they're hobbies."

—JON STEWART

Values are the spiritual principles and beliefs that govern our actions. They are internal guidelines that determine our priorities and let us know when we're living in sync with what we feel is most important to us.

When our actions match our values, we experience a feeling of congruence, a sense of harmony and peace. But when our actions are out of alignment with our value system, we instead feel a sense of unhappiness, anxiety, and despair. We may end up using addictions to mask this inner turmoil, trying to numb and silence our inner voice. We may become physically ill or suffer from mental illnesses such as depression or anxiety. Our relationships may suffer, and we may find ourselves surrounded by people who reflect this lack of alignment and inner chaos.

We mistakenly believe that our values are flexible and relative to the situation. But with time and experience, we usually find that our values are innate, unique to us, like our DNA or our fingerprints. Learning to recognize our own values and build our lives around honoring them can mean the difference between ease and tranquility and stress, conflict, and confusion.

So, how can you determine your core values? Well, first think back to the times in your life when you were the most content, fulfilled, and proud. What were you doing? Where were you? Who were you with? What were the circumstances? What was the occasion? Why did you feel so happy? What made you feel proud? How did these experiences provide your life with meaning and purpose?

Write down the answers to these questions and review the results. If you find you are writing about time spent in nature, yet you work in a closed off indoor location that suffocates you, you may have to seriously reconsider your choice of employment. Similarly, if you are writing about acting, singing, performing, and dancing, yet you work in an office doing left-brained activities, it might be time to reevaluate your choices. By getting clear on our values, we can examine our life choices in a new light, measuring them against our newly defined internal compass.

The following is a list of values from MindTools.com. Which are in your top ten?

Accountability	Altruism	Being the best
Accuracy	Ambition	Belonging
Achievement	Assertiveness	Boldness
Adventurousness	Balance	Calmness

Carefulness	Devoutness	Fitness
Challenge	Diligence	Fluency
Cheerfulness	Discipline	Focus
Clear-mindedness	Discretion	Freedom
Commitment	Diversity	Fun
Community	Dynamism	Generosity
Compassion	Economy	Goodness
Competitiveness	Effectiveness	Grace
Consistency	Efficiency	Growth
Contentment	Elegance	Happiness
Continuous Improvement	Empathy	Hard Work
	Enjoyment	Health
Contribution	Enthusiasm	Helping Society
Control	Equality	Holiness
Cooperation	Excellence	Honesty
Correctness	Excitement	Honor
Courtesy	Expertise	Humility
Creativity	Exploration	Independence
Curiosity	Expressiveness	Ingenuity
Decisiveness	Fairness	Inner Harmony
Democraticness	Faith	Inquisitiveness
Dependability	Family-orientedness	Insightfulness
Determination	Fidelity	Intelligence

Intellectual Status

Intuition

Joy

Justice

Leadership

Legacy

Love

Loyalty

Making a
    difference

Mastery

Merit

Obedience

Openness

Order

Originality

Patriotism

Perfection

Piety

Positivity

Practicality

Preparedness

Professionalism

Prudence

Quality-orientation

Reliability

Resourcefulness

Restraint

Results-oriented

Rigor

Security

Self-actualization

Self-control

Selflessness

Self-reliance

Sensitivity

Serenity

Service

Shrewdness

Simplicity

Soundness

Speed

Spontaneity

Stability

Strategic

Strength

Structure

Success

Support

Teamwork

Temperance

Thankfulness

Thoroughness

Thoughtfulness

Timeliness

Tolerance

Traditionalism

Trustworthiness

Truth-seeking

Understanding

Uniqueness

Unity

Usefulness

Vision

Vitality

EARLY DOUBLE BINDS AND SUPPRESSED VALUES

For many of us, we begin our lives with our values intact, but then our early experiences force us to stray from what we care about most. For instance, we may have been born with the desire to have a lot of fun, but if we grew up in a totalitarian-like household with strict rules and a lot of punishment, we may have been forced to abandon that core value in exchange for the values of our caregivers.

This is what is known as a "double bind." It means a situation in which our loyalty is pulled in two opposite directions. We have a need to be true to ourselves, yet we also have a need to survive, and one of those must win. We choose survival, yet live with the ache of having subdued our need for self-expression.

In order to survive, especially in dysfunctional childhoods, we may have had to subvert our values in favor of adopting those around us so many times that we lose a connection to ourselves entirely. We may feel totally lost, not knowing what we really care about or what really drives our passion. We may simply have never been afforded the time, respect, space, or freedom needed to really explore our values growing up, and now find ourselves comprised of bits and pieces of everyone else—but with nothing authentically our own.

Reactive Core Values

Not everyone responds to a difficult childhood by straying from their values, however. Many times, our core values solidify as a result of a traumatic past. For instance, we may have grown up poor, and thus as adults have the core value of being driven, ambitious, and entrepreneurial. Perhaps we grew up in a violent neighborhood where people were always fighting. This may have led us to develop the core value of peacefulness, because we experienced firsthand how challenging life was without it.

Double Binds and Addiction

Addiction itself is directly related to our value system. Addiction serves to numb our pain and trauma, and the need to continue numbing may outweigh our desire for integrity. For instance, we may end up stealing, lying, and cheating to obtain our fix, knowing full well that we don't feel right inside about those things. Yet we do them anyways because of the double bind of needing to medicate our pain.

The problem is that, while on the one hand we may have achieved partial numbness with an addictive substance or behavior, we now have to deal with the pain that comes from ignoring our value systems. This is why addiction is unsustainable and only leads to greater suffering than the one we're trying to cover up.

VALUES TO LIVE BY

The great leaders of our times all exhibit the core universal values of integrity, passion, confidence, and perseverance, among others. From Oprah Winfrey, Steve Jobs, and Abraham Lincoln to Simone Biles, JK Rowling, and Muhammad Ali, greatness begins with an unwavering adherence to one's personal code of ethics.

As we explore each of these values below, think about how each is active or non-active in your life today. Are there certain values you recognize, but find hard to implement? Do you experience a double bind of having to be loyal to others' values while forgoing your own so you don't lose your job, your relationship, or your social standing? Are you afraid to rock the boat? Do you shy away from expressing your core values to better blend in and people-please? Ask yourself, in what ways you are compromising and how can you be more authentic in your expression of your true guiding values, starting today?

Integrity

The word integrity comes from "integer," meaning whole or complete. It equates with being whole inside, practicing honesty, consistency, and trustworthiness. Integrity is visible through our actions, words, and decisions. It means doing the right thing, even when there isn't any apparent gain for doing so. It means doing the right thing, even when no one is watching.

It also means that we place others' well-being above our own selfish desires. If we make mistakes, we admit them. If others make mistakes, we do our best to forgive them. We treat everyone equally, rather than granting special favors to certain groups. Integrity is the foundation for healthy relationships, whether personal, business, or family-related.

In what ways do you practice integrity? In what instances has your integrity been compromised, and why? Were there any double binds at work that caused you to abandon this value, even temporarily? Who in your life do you consider to have integrity, and have you told them lately how highly you think of them?

Passion

Passion is a word that describes a great love and enthusiasm for something, a love that borders on the obsessive and is far more dedicated than a mere hobby level. Passion inspires the desire to spend countless hours perfecting a skill, working at a business, or practicing an instrument. Passion is the "fire" within you that burns so bright, others notice and respond and are instantly converted to your cause.

Passion demands investment, sacrifice, and commitment. It often begins in childhood and continues until old age. It drives you to keep going, regardless of setbacks, criticism, or rejection. Passion doesn't care about those things because the joy it brings is irrefutable.

What is it that brings you passion in life? If you haven't felt it in a while, why haven't you? What keeps you from expressing your passion? What experiences or events have dimmed your fire and made you push your passion to take a back seat to more practical matters? What can you do today to bring passion back into your life and keep it there?

Excellence

Excellence is a word that gets used a lot in business settings, but it needn't only apply to work. It is a quality of striving for the highest possible standards, meticulously attending to every detail and polishing to perfection. Excellence means assessing and reassessing to ensure no stone has been left unturned to achieve the goal.

Implied in the quality of excellence is an inherent discipline and focus, followed up with continuous action. Excellence can be employed in a simple task such as cleaning one's room, or in a grand accomplishment such as performing a concerto on the piano. In short, excellence is more about our attitude towards what we do rather than the act itself.

When and where do you practice excellence in your life? Were you ever shamed for doing "too good" a job on something, and learned to "dumb it down?" Have you ever been led to hide your excellence from the world in order to fit in with more mediocrity? Did you feel out of place trying your hardest, surrounded by slackers and people who were too "cool" to care? How can you celebrate those around you who practice excellence today?

Responsibility

The concept of responsibility is something we are encouraged to learn early on in our lives, as it is a prerequisite for almost any type of employment or relationship. It means doing what you say you are going to do and accepting the consequences if you fail to keep your word. It means being reliable and consistent and receiving others' trust. Responsibility builds character and helps us to become stronger and more confident.

If you are struggling with responsibility in your life, it may be because you were not provided with a proper example of it as a kid. If you grew up with irresponsible, chaotic caregivers who couldn't be trusted, you may not grasp the meaning of responsibility in the first place. The joy of commitment may elude you because you have simply never known stability in your home of origin.

You may be gripped by a fear of inadequacy that causes you to avoid responsibility entirely. You may be terrified of letting people down, of being a fraud, or of being inept.

But the thing about responsibility is that we're never ready for it until after we assume it. Ask anyone who has had a child. They rise to the occasion, because responsibility itself is what ennobles us and lifts us into a realm of connectedness we have not known before. You leap first, then look.

Commitment

Commitment is similar to responsibility in that it refines our character and enriches our lives. It means making a decision and sticking with it, no matter what obstacles appear in our paths to discourage us.

A romantic relationship or marriage is a commitment, one which requires us to go through both good and bad times without quitting when things get rough. Having a child is another commitment that we make, to love and support another human being who is totally dependent on us.

The word "commitment" can be very scary for some people, but this is generally because they have never experienced the benefits and joy that commitment can bring. For instance, making the decision to graduate from college can lead to tremendous pride and self-esteem, despite all the hard work and personal sacrifice it may require. Having a dog is another commitment that at first may seem daunting, considering all the cleanup, vet visits, costs, and attention required, but it is a commitment that pays off far beyond what is demanded.

All this being said, it's still important to evaluate each situation in light of self-care, as not everything is worth sticking with. There are certain people who are so committed to their job that they will continue working in a toxic, abusive environment rather than quit to look for something else. Others over-commit to relationships and don't know how to leave when things become unhealthy.

Knowing when, how, and why to commit is a process each person must learn to navigate for themselves. Working with a therapist or counselor can be invaluable in helping to determine when to stay and when to go in many of our everyday circumstances.

Confidence

Confidence can be defined as the feeling that you will be successful in achieving that which you set out to do, whether it's dancing, finding a dating partner, solving the world's dire problems, or ice skating for the first time. Confidence isn't always based on proven skill or acumen; it can be based merely on a rock-solid belief in yourself that no one can refute.

Some people envy those with confidence, believing it to be something you're born with or something you grow up with. Good news—anyone at all can decide to have confidence, and presto, they have it! It is all about attitude, a state of mind, and a decision to overcome any obstacles placed in one's path without hesitation.

Confidence is not necessarily about building yourself up with empty, unrealistic praise. Rather, it is the idea that you can handle anything and have what it takes to improve at things you are not yet good at. Confidence tells you that it is possible to learn on the job, to acquire new experiences and to be enriched by them.

Creative visualization is an especially useful tool for creating confidence. If you can visualize yourself succeeding before attempting a task, you are far more likely to achieve your goal. Athletes visualize scoring a goal before they go out on the field, and actors visualize receiving a standing ovation before going out on stage. Even if you are just planning to out someone out on a date, visualizing a favorable response can increase your confidence tremendously.

People who grew up in abusive or dysfunctional households may struggle with their confidence, having been yelled at repeatedly or told they were not good enough. Over time, they may have taken these false-hoods to heart and started to doubt themselves deeply. What's remarkable about the human brain, however, is that it can quickly establish new pathways in the opposite direction with simple repetition. By repeatedly telling yourself you are smart, capable, talented, loveable, and successful, your brain gradually rewires itself and starts to produce the "chemicals of success."

Listening to positive messages in guided meditation, posting notes of encouragement around your house, and surrounding yourself with only the most loving, kind people in your life are all highly effective in working to reverse early self-defeating patterns.

Perseverance

Have you ever run a marathon, or knew someone who did? Running 26.3 miles requires the value of perseverance. Perseverance is the relentless drive to see a task through to the end, whether it's climbing a mountain or finishing college.

Winners, athletic or otherwise, all have perseverance. It is the ability to weather setbacks, to keep pushing, no matter how many times you are knocked down. Sometimes perseverance is more important than intelligence, talent, or privilege. Sometimes it is that one ingredient that guarantees your success.

Compassion

Exercising compassion means showing kindness and empathy towards everyone you encounter. Rather than running people over on your way to the top, you stop to value and appreciate each person's contribution to your journey. Compassion is an authentic desire to help others, rather than exploit them as a means to an end.

Compassion demands that we put ourselves in others' shoes and try to walk a mile. It means giving others the benefit of the doubt while seeking to understand those that offend us, rather than judge and reject them.

Rather than keeping us down, compassion actually lifts us up by strengthening our relationships, both professional and personal, and creating more positive, supportive environments in which everyone thrives. Businesses are slowly finding that more compassion in the workplace actually boosts the bottom line instead of impeding it.

Patience

Patience is a hard one for many of us. We live in a culture of instant gratification and accelerated relationships. Everything is at our fingertips, and we value getting things done yesterday, if not sooner. Hardly anyone has time anymore for a nice, slow-cooked meal, both literally and figuratively.

We find ourselves short on patience, whether it's when we're dealing with electronics or when we're dating. We can't slow down, and so we end up jumping from task to task, from person to person, or from job to job. Chronic discontentment drives us to constantly trade in the old for the new.

Learning patience, however, is essential for achieving anything truly worthwhile in life, from a marriage, to playing an instrument, to getting a promotion at work. If we know ahead of time to expect the long haul, we can be more at ease and better handle the ups and downs. Patience is cultivated through the frustrations we face on a daily basis, both mundane and profound.

Gratitude

I have saved gratitude for last because it is among the most important of human values. When we choose the perspective of gratitude and make it the foundation of our approach towards life, each day becomes a true delight rather than a chore. Gratitude is like the elixir that turns our complaints, frustrations, and entitlements into harmless dust while reminding us of how love is what really matters in this life.

Gratitude shows us that each person, place, and thing is our teacher, and that even if we have suffered, we may have learned a valuable lesson we can be thankful for. Our hardships, trauma, and abuse can all become a source of inner strength with which we can inspire, help, and uplift other survivors. What doesn't kill us makes us stronger, as the old saying goes.

We practice gratitude when we pay it forward, giving back what we have receive from others in this life. Gratitude reminds us how lucky we are and shows us how much we have to offer others, even if we might not think so.

Taking the Next Step

I have compiled twenty affirmations to help you reaffirm your deepest life values and get back on track when you fall short. Learning to live in alignment with your beliefs is a process, not a destination, so you don't have to be perfect—you only have to try. You can print these affirmations and hang them in your office or home, or you can simply read them in this book, knowing they are already beginning to work in your life.

Affirmations for Values

- I find it easy to keep my promises.
- I am aligned with my highest values and live accordingly.
- My life is filled with passion.
- I open my heart and let love in.
- I strive for excellence in all that I do.
- I am confident in my choices and in who I am.
- I am resilient and persevering, no matter how hard things get.
- I practice compassion towards myself and others.
- I am patient and know that good things come to those who wait.
- I practice daily gratitude for all the good in my life.
- My actions and my values are perfectly aligned.
- My values give my life deep meaning and purpose.
- I take the time to get to know myself fully.
- Today I will stand up for what I believe in.
- I take time each day to reflect on what I believe in most.
- I set aside my selfishness and focus on helping others.
- I stay true to my personal code of honor.
- I am proud of the person I have become.
- I am focused and clear about my life goals.
- I express my values in all my words and actions.

Chapter 10

EVOLUTION

"Don't live the same day over and over again and call that a life. Life is about evolving mentally, spiritually, and emotionally."

—GERMANY KENT

Change, growth, and evolution are all innate facets of being alive. From plants and animals to entire ecosystems, every living thing is in a constant process of evolving. Nothing stays static or stagnant. Yet as human beings, we can sometimes fall into a rut where we refuse to move forward and refuse to change our ways.

We may try to resist our own evolution through addiction, isolation, or other self-destructive behaviors, but ultimately doing so will only make change, which *is* inevitable, more difficult for ourselves. Everyone must grow up sooner or later, and by learning to embrace the process of personal growth we can learn to enjoy our transformation rather than dread it.

GROWTH AS A WAY OF LIFE

Healthy people understand that growing, learning, and evolving is a process that never ends. There are always more books to read, more classes to take, more life skills to gain. Once we think of evolution as a lifestyle, we can begin to embrace change as a normal part of our day and less as something we do just in response to a crisis.

A business that stops growing and expanding becomes stagnant and cannot sustain itself. Similarly, if we as people decide to stop making new friends, stop asking questions about the way things work, or stop questioning the political process, we are prone to falling into a rut.

Ruts are often sustained by some kind of addiction, such as bingeing on candy, watching too much TV, watching too much porn, smoking cigarettes, or shopping compulsively. Addictions keep us locked into a routine that never changes, stunting our own growth so that we never truly unfurl to our full height, never fully command our true potential. We live in "what might have been," always stuck wondering what we could have achieved if we had dared.

EVOLUTION AND OUR PHYSICAL HEALTH

To grow healthy bones and muscles as young people, we have to stretch, run, play, jump, fall down, and leap into the sky. Building a healthy body requires movement, risk, and discomfort.

But once we get to adulthood, we often become stagnant physically. We may get a job at a desk, start munching on chips, and just forget about taking physical risks altogether, settling into a lifestyle of sitting on the couch after work, watching TV before rolling into bed.

This type of sedentary lifestyle is ultimately not sustainable. We have to keep exercising and evolving physically in order to meet the challenges of life and old age. By doing yoga, lifting weights, hiking, swimming, running, or doing martial arts, we keep our spines active and avoid succumbing to diseases later in life, such as osteoporosis or obesity. We only get one body, so it's important to keep challenging it with new, interesting activities that balance out the time we spend looking at screens, online, and using our phones.

EVOLUTION AND OUR MENTAL HEALTH

Just like our bodies need exercise, so, too, do our minds. Keeping mentally sharp with puzzles, reading books, and learning new skills is mandatory for avoiding fogginess, dementia, and forgetfulness in older years. We have to continuously challenge ourselves mentally to stay agile, by looking at things from different angles, thinking critically, and asking questions about things we don't understand.

Evolution is an essential ingredient in combatting mental illnesses such as depression and anxiety. I know one woman who got herself out of a deep depression when her father died unexpectedly by challenging herself to run a half-marathon, even though she had never run before. By funneling all her grief and rage into her training, she was able to make the most of her suffering, evolving into an athlete and choosing health over despair.

DETACHING FROM THOSE THAT HOLD US BACK

Change is something that every dysfunctional family fears. In a toxic environment, everyone has a role and must remain as a fixture in order to perpetuate the unhealthy dynamic. If one person begins to evolve, transform, and grow, it sends out a ripple effect, putting everyone else's steady-state into jeopardy.

The toxic family may therefore take measures to clip the wings of anyone who dares attempt evolution. If one grew up in such a situation, there can be no doubt that change becomes difficult and frightening, especially if it was initially met with punishment, shame, rejection, or violence in younger years.

The toxic situation need not come from childhood, either. It may be a job, a group of friends, a club, or a relationship that requires us to maintain the status quo. Change will always be a threat to those who are more comfortable with complacency and apathy. If we begin to evolve, we may feel that we are choosing to distance ourselves from those around us that are holding us back. This can be a lonely feeling, which is why so many of us avoid our own transformation.

What we may not understand is that by choosing growth, we open ourselves up to a whole new world of friends and supporters who want the best for us, who accept us as evolved individuals, and who are thrilled for us as we continue to transform into our highest, most actualized selves.

These are the people that want us to lose the weight, support us in getting a new job, even if it's far away, who want to see us find love, and who want to see us pursue our dreams, no matter how "foolish" they appear. These types of friends are secure enough to let us blossom and shine because they themselves are doing so, too.

SEEKING OUT POSITIVE ROLE MODELS

Positive role models function as butterflies do before caterpillars. Seeing a butterfly high in the sky with its beautiful wings gives the caterpillar the faith that all its hard work won't be for nothing.

We all need butterflies in our lives to maintain our faith in beauty, hope, and transcendence. These butterflies may be famous people who you respect, people you met in childhood who showed you respect, or fictional people who you admire and hope to emulate. I once knew a man who hung pictures of both Jimi Hendrix and Bruce Lee around his house to inspire him towards greater strength, creativity, and virtuosity every day.

Finding mentors who have done exactly what you want to do is also a great step for moving forward with your dreams and goals. Sometimes just having coffee with someone successful in your field can make you feel included and motivated, even if all that happens is that you get a glimpse of that person's humanity.

You will be surprised by how many successful people are eager to give back to others and help an up-and-coming artist or businessperson out. When we come from small-minded families or backgrounds, we can imagine everyone is the jealous, withholding, petty type. But this is not the case; the world is literally filled with generous, open, kind people who want nothing more than to support us in being our best.

So take a risk, and reach out to a potential mentor working in your dream profession. If you want to be married, ask someone who is happily married how they did it. If you want to be a musician, go to a show and stay behind to chat with the performers and ask they if they have any tips for someone just starting out. All it takes is courage, but the results can catapult you forwards exponentially.

WORKING THROUGH FEARS

Fear is among the biggest roadblocks to evolution in one's life. Fear is the universal obstacle that holds so many of us back from stepping forward into the unknown, daring to fulfill our personal destinies. It shuts us down before we've even made an attempt, telling us not to bother trying. It warns us of consequences beyond our control while belittling our attempts.

Despite its negative consequences, fear is very natural and normal for human beings. It exists within us as a defense against being hurt. Healthy fear is what prevents us from jumping from great heights, burning ourselves on a stove, or walking alone in a dangerous neighborhood at night.

In healthy families, a child is given ample chance to differentiate between healthy fear and the type of fear that can be overcome through action. In these supportive environments, a child is encouraged to take risks and build self-esteem and self-confidence while overcoming all kinds of everyday fears, from fear of the dark to fear of looking foolish.

But not all of us were fortunate enough to grow up in a situation that gave us the opportunity to work through our fear. Many of us entered adulthood still terrified of failure, being laughed at, or being rejected. We may have even experienced these negative reactions to our goals from our primary caregivers. We may be so used to living in fear that we don't even realize it's fear; instead, we just see fear as "reality."

As adults, we may have to re-parent ourselves, rewiring our brains to act despite our fears, knowing that on the other side is something much more thrilling, meaningful, and surprising. To evolve, we must comfort ourselves through the difficult process of shedding our fears, knowing that they are only shadows and that, with every step forward, we are coming into the light.

The Fear of Being Hurt Again

If you have been hurt, whether through abuse, abandonment, betrayal, or even self-sabotage, it makes sense that you feel afraid to move forward in your life. It may actually seem safer to stay stuck in a rut rather than risk feeling that pain all over again. For instance, those who went through a bad breakup or divorce may be so scared of being hurt again that they don't date and don't allow love in their lives, instead settling for a safe, but very shut down, existence.

Another person may have tried to start a business years ago and failed and felt humiliated in front of friends and family. Now, stuck at a dead-end job they dislike, this person refuses to attempt a new business idea because they would rather avoid looking foolish again. They may not understand that most successful business owners started two or three businesses before they found the one that was profitable. Instead of continuing to evolve, this person shuts down, choosing to live a safe but ultimately unrewarding life.

Grieving the loss of our plans, hopes, and dreams is the first step towards restoring our faith in the future. We need to understand that just because one person hurt us, it doesn't mean the next person will. We need to lick our wounds while finding a way to start over, knowing that the future is a clean slate. What happened in the past does not define us. We can write our story from the present moment, because all the power is in the present.

The Fear of the Unknown

Another common driving fear is the fear of the unknown. We feel safer doing what we've always done, following our routine without rocking the boat. Change is frightening because we don't know what the outcome will be. If we've always been overweight, for example, we may avoid losing the pounds just because we can't imagine what we'll feel like in a different body. If we've always lived in a small town, we may choose to stay there because we cannot envision living anywhere else.

The thing about the unknown is that the second you throw yourself into it, it stops being the unknown and becomes "the known." Everyone who has ever moved to a new city was a stranger at first, until about a year later when they became a native and learned their way around by heart. If you've never done stand-up comedy before, it can feel like the great unknown—until you get up there and do it, that is. Then you become an authority on it.

To overcome the fear of the unknown, we need to recapture that childlike sense of adventure from when we dreamed of flying into space on a spaceship or living in a castle and being a princess. We had all these kinds of fantasies, dreams about scenarios we had never been in, and they filled us with excitement. As adults, we can tap into that wonder and sense of delight and try to see taking risks as something fun again, rather than something to dread.

The Fear of Failure

Fear of failure is easy to understand—no one likes to fail! It sucks. It's embarrassing and depressing. But most successful people know that in order to succeed, we first have to fail many, many times. Those that acclimate themselves to this fact dig in and start failing, often and with gusto. They refuse to be discouraged, and just keep failing their little hearts out until they finally hit the jackpot.

This is exactly how the airplane, telephone, and lightbulb were all invented. Anyone who works in sales knows the value of failure and rejection. For every individual sale, there may be as many as fifty "no's." And anyone who ever played professional baseball knows that hitting a home run is impossible without striking out over and over. In the same year that Babe Ruth broke the record for most home runs scored, he also broke the record for the most strikeouts. He struck out more than any other player because he didn't view striking out as a setback or anything to be ashamed of. He simply saw it as "playing the game."

If you weren't afraid to fail, what would you be doing with your life? If you knew you had to fail again and again to succeed, would it take some of the sting out of it? Would you be a little less afraid to play a wrong note, draw a bad picture, strike out, mess up, get rejected, or be booed offstage if you knew that it had happened to nearly every famous person you've heard of?

The script for the original *Rocky* film, written by Sylvester Stallone in 1976, was rejected over 1500 times by producers and directors. Stallone persevered until he found the one film company who would make the movie with him as the lead actor, even though his face was half-para-lyzed and he slurred his speech slightly. The film went on to gross $225 million at the box office, and to this very day is still inspiring sequels, including the latest one, *Creed*, helmed by the director of Black Panther.

Rocky is an incredible success story, one that reminds us that we don't know the number of rejections we may face before success. That number may be ten, or it may be 1000, but if we keep believing in ourselves, people will eventually come around to our point of view. It is inevitable. So long as we refuse to go home until we achieve our goal, the Universe will support us.

The Fear of Success

Less common, and slightly more complex, is fear of failure's cousin, success. Fear of success can be just as devastating and debilitating as fear of failure. We may be afraid to succeed because in our childhood homes we were given the message that it isn't okay to outshine our parents or siblings. We may have been a gifted child in an environment where being exceptional was equated with haughtiness or a superiority complex. We may have heard statements such as, "Who do she think she is?" that were designed to make us think twice before standing out from the pack.

Other kids grow up in homes where their talents are used by their parents to punish another sibling. Jimmy might be told, "Why can't you be more like Jamie, who gets an A on every test?" This hurts Jimmy, but it also hurts Jamie, who grows up believing that when he succeeds, it hurts others. For this reason, he may spend his life hiding his intelligence from others, lest it be used to humiliate another loved one.

If we were abused as children, the perpetrators may have used our talents or good looks to single us out, showering us with compliments to win us over so that they could exploit us. In these cases, we may grow up mistakenly believing that it was our talent that caused us to be abused. We end up abandoning all that is amazing about us, choosing instead to downplay our skills or our beauty so we won't be singled out again.

Children who were sexually abused often believe it was their sexiness or beauty that caused the crime. They may develop eating disorders to cover their bodies with protective layers of fat or eat so little that they have no curves. Children in these situations may develop poor hygiene and avoid socializing. Any situation where they may be favored or put in the spotlight or "liked" is avoided, because those things are associated with sexual abuse. This person will have a long struggle ahead of them to learn to own their beauty, sexuality, and talent—to be proud of those things and place the blame squarely on the perpetrator's shoulders, rather than their own.

Overcoming fear of success requires the love and support of a community that accepts us unconditionally, no matter how well or poorly we do. Building this support network is invaluable in healing the wounds of isolation and hiding. Often, finding others with the same fears helps us to put them in perspective and move forward.

The Fear of Growing Up

While most kids and teenagers long for the day when they can achieve their independence, learn to drive, get a job, and leave home, not every young person feels this way. Some younger people are terrified of growing up because it means losing the security, safety and familiarity of home.

Their family may consider them "babies" and give them the impression that growing up means being abandoned. In this case, the person will stunt their own growth to avoid losing the approval and love of their unhealthy caregivers. Being strong, independent, and autonomous may be seen as a threat to dysfunctional parents, who desire to keep their child under their thumb forever.

For this person, growing up and evolving will mean risking being alone. They will have to accept that being coddled, enabled, and over-protected is not the same thing as being loved. Real love means supporting our dear ones, helping them be the best they can be—fully independent, high-functioning adults with their own lives and relationships outside of the nuclear family.

Taking the Next Step

Evolution begins the moment you make the decision to work on your life and make changes. And it continues as you read this chapter, releasing your own inner blocks to success and happiness. To help, here are twenty affirmations on the topic of evolution for you to work with on your journey.

Affirmations for Evolution

- I am constantly evolving—mentally, physically, emotionally, and spiritually.
- My spiritual life is evolving, bringing peace and forgiveness.
- I am courageously transforming on a daily basis.
- I now allow myself to grow up.
- I take the risk to grow and evolve.
- My life is unfolding in perfect timing.
- I own my power and use it for good.
- I always have the expectation of success.
- I can achieve whatever I put my mind to.
- I now allow my talents and intelligence to blossom.
- I release all negative, unsupportive people from my life.
- I focus my efforts on doing the very best that I can.
- I am a vibrant source of inspiration to others.
- I follow my heart and pursue my dreams.
- I listen to my intuition and inner wisdom.
- Today, I will seek out positive role models who energize me.
- Today, I will take the risk to love again.
- I now release all fear of the unknown.
- I now release my fear of success.
- I now release my fear of failure.

Chapter 11

TECHNOLOGY

"Technology is best when it brings people together."

—MATT MULLENWEG

As humankind has progressed, our technological feats have soared higher and higher. We have been able to elevate the fields of medicine, art, travel, national defense, and so many more industries through innovative improvements that we all take for granted today. There is no one aspect of our lives that hasn't been greatly advanced by technological achievements.

Unfortunately, our emotional response and responsibility are lagging behind. We are just now learning to adjust to the idea of robots or AI and their implications in our workforce. We are just beginning to understand how to balance the ability to communicate with anyone, anytime, with the need for our precious privacy, solitude, and connection with the Earth. And our journey will continue even as the tech sector continues to wow us with new inventions.

Technology *can* be a tool for living a full, purposeful life with meaningful relationships—or it can be a means of staying small, maintaining an existence whose focus is the blue glow of a computer or smartphone screen. That would be nothing short of tragic. There's too much beauty in the world, and we each have such infinite possibility that we all owe it to ourselves to choose the brighter path.

TECHNOLOGY AND INTEGRITY

The word "integrity" has two definitions. The first definition relates to being honest and morally upright. Of course, this is desirable behavior in general. But the integrity that we refer to here is defined as "the state of being whole and undivided." Disappearing into hours of internet usage, if it's not productive and is purely for escape, fragments an individual. It causes us to press "pause" on interacting with other people and the world in a meaningful way. It stands in the way of our developing a healthy, authentic self.

It can be easy for us to hide out in our "work," spending hours and hours online in a virtual environment, all under the guise of productivity. We can claim to be an "aficionado" or connoisseur of a certain topic, such as literature, music, or film, and hide from reality by delving deeper and deeper into online archives. These are modern day postures that can be afforded some legitimacy but are really just fancy ways of checking out and avoiding human intimacy.

In fact, addiction to technology, while a less-explored area of dysfunction than alcoholism, eating disorders, or gambling, is yet disturbing the lives of so many of our young people who have grown up immersed in an online existence. It can be easy for older generations to look the other way since the nuances of technology elude them, but this is a grave mistake. Younger people may not have the interpersonal tools that older folks were forced to develop in an age before social media, texting, or even email, so they can benefit greatly from being around people born in the 50's, 60's and 70's.

THE DIGITAL SELF

The Digital Self is the term I use for our online presence. It's a wholly separate identity from who we are in real life. At one end of the scale, it's a relatively honest extension of our day-to-day lives, comprised of snapshots of designs seen in the foam of our cappuccino, or a work-weary proclamation of "TGIF" when the weekend arrives. For people with regular nine-to-five jobs who aren't using social media to market a business or side career, this is pretty common.

Then, there is the tireless self-marketer who may be promoting an actual business, or the individual who is simply compelled to document and share everything 24/7. This person may be neglecting their exercise, sleep, friendships, or other forms of self-care because their digital self is so active online.

At the dishonest end of the spectrum, there are people whose online existence is a complete falsehood, including "catfish"—people pursuing online romance under a totally false identity. There is a part of them that craves interaction but believes they cannot participate in the world on honest terms.

Most of us don't go that far, but consider: when we present ourselves online, do we routinely leave out the more vulnerable or human aspects of our personality? Do we instead choose to present only our most shin-ing moments of victory? And does this not perpetuate a culture of "com-pare and despair?" We may not be outright lying online, but many of us participate in "lies of omission" by manipulating our digital stories to only reflect a self we believe others will envy. This behavior can really thin the fabric of our relationships and isolate us, even on a platform whose purpose is to bring us closer together.

THE ROLE OF TECHNOLOGY IN BUILDING INTIMACY AND RELATIONSHIPS

Gone are the "swinging singles" bars of yesteryear. Or else, if they're still around, people are just sitting at the bar, staring at their phones. People are meeting online so often that there's barely any stigma anymore to saying, "We met on Match." In fact, I believe that we've arrived at the converse: meeting in real life is the anomaly.

But the digital age has created a new set of barriers for maintaining relationships. The constant consumption of TV and films, which has become ingrained as part of people's thinking, has fostered unrealistic expectations for what a happy relationship is supposed to look like. Fictional romances ignite, explode, and burn out all within a maximum of ninety minutes, while real life must aim for something more sustainable, long-term.

Further complicating matters is how online dating has created endless "possibilities," so that one can always "upgrade" with a swipe of the thumb. We've pushed aside the emotional intelligence and vulnerability necessary to weather conflict. Ubiquitous online technology has also given rise to a new breed of infidelity: the online, "emotional" affair.

The boldness of asking for someone's number—or giving it to someone—and risking rejection is gone. It has been replaced by wild extremes of aloofness and expectations of sex after exchanging a few messages. The new social dynamic also allows for numerous ways to experience micro-rejections: for example, saying, "We both swiped right but he didn't message me."

Sometimes people treat online dating like a video game, passing the time in a way where the goal is to be chosen but not necessarily to meet in person. It presents a new level of safety concerns now that you are literally meeting a stranger from the internet. How do you maintain an openness to romantic possibility while maintaining your physical and emotional safety?

Learning to take the good aspects of online dating—the ability to come into contact with a wide variety of interesting people from all areas—and couple them with a more human, intimacy-building approach, i.e. courting in person, limiting texting, and insisting on face-to-face contact, is challenging but doable. It simply takes refining our intentions and having the courage to go out of our comfort zones a little more often.

It means balancing our online pursuits with some in-person events and mixers and remaining open to connecting with others everywhere we go, whether it's to do the laundry, to jury duty, or to take a hike in nature. Love is everywhere, if we're sincere about finding it.

CYBER BULLYING

Children who have been born into a world with social media are uniquely vulnerable to bullying in ways that adults who grew up in previous generations weren't. The horror stories of children who have been "trolled" by their classmates are sadly familiar. Some have been taunted and teased so relentlessly that they end up committing suicide or resort to addiction or self-harm. Teens have had their sexual activities filmed against their will and then live-streamed to thousands. That kind of humiliation and abuse is inconceivable to those of us who grew up in the age of AOL and dial-up connections.

We may think, "Why don't they just stay offline?" but this is no longer a real possibility for a young person living in a world where every single one of their peers is digitally active. In fact, many of their classes are taught online; their teachers may even require them to participate in Facebook groups, for instance. It can be more difficult than we realize to avoid bullying—bullying that we would never tolerate if it were in the form of physical threats or violence.

Unfortunately, it's also alarmingly common for adults to engage in these antisocial behaviors, aiming threats and obscenities at public figures or everyday people using online platform. People will say things on Yelp, for instance, that they would never dare utter in person. The internet has brought out the ugliest parts of human nature and then normalized them under the banner of "free speech."

Monitoring and patrolling online platforms is the duty of any company that operates digitally, just as schools and public spaces are patrolled by security guards. We have to learn to treat our online spaces just as seriously as we do our actual environments, blocking those who use hate speech or bully others. By creating digital equivalents of our real-world safety protocols, we can eventually protect digital spaces—or at least significantly improve it.

As parents, we need to get beyond our fears of infringing on our children's individuality and recognize it is our duty to meticulously comb through their contacts to protect them from predators. It's also important to create an atmosphere of trust and disclosure at home so that our kids will come to us with problems rather than confide in strangers or choose negative coping mechanisms.

If someone is bullying you online, there's a lot you can do to fight back. Remember first that it is not your fault. You can take screenshots of the interactions, learn how to utilize your privacy settings, and report harassers who cross the line. The common address for reporting abuse is abuse@websitename.com, where "websitename" refers to whichever platform or company you'd like to report to.

All of us need to use empathy to understand that there are consequences to our actions, words, and deeds, in both real space and the digital space. There are human beings on the other end of our keystrokes with feelings, who can experience real and lasting pain from our actions if they're harmful. We have to fight against the numbness that online activity can sometimes bring and engage in healthy, respectful exchanges, regardless of the medium.

TECHNOLOGY AND MAINTAINING A DAILY SPIRITUAL CONNECTION

The lure of staring at our phones is powerful. The compulsion to check out mentally and just run on auto-pilot is something that has been with us well before the advent of computers. With that in mind, we need something powerful and consistent to counterbalance this tendency. That can be anything that's powerful, grounding, and bigger than us.

"Spiritual" doesn't necessarily mean "religious," although it can be. It can be a daily walk around the block, being in nature, making a point of talking to someone you care about, or just sitting quietly and surrendering all our internal chatter.

A spiritual connection will help reset a lot of the negative thinking that can permeate our consciousness. If forging a spiritual connection is new to you, it may elicit the thought that "I'm doing it wrong." Pushing past that is where growth lies.

Try to spend just part of your day, each day, entirely "unplugged." This forces you to be present and connect with your environment and the people around you. You may make a new friend or see a magnificent sunset that makes your jaw drop. And maybe just this once, try to receive it as a gift from the Universe without succumbing to the compulsion to share it on Instagram.

SOCIAL MEDIA: THE GOOD, THE BAD AND THE UGLY

That said, I love seeing what my young niece posts on Instagram. Before my eyes, she's becoming a funny, creative, and bright young woman. Recently, I was with her when she posted a photo of a turtle she saw on vacation in Hawaii. It made her happy to share it … until she saw that it only received nine "likes."

Her whole energy changed when she admitted this to me. This dynamic encapsulates the entire pendulum of social media. We experience the joy of connecting with people we know in real life who now live far away as well as "meeting" people all over the world. We've also receive an emotional boost from lots of people liking what we post and responding positively.

But many of us also feel the sense that we aren't enough when we don't get the mass embrace we feel we should be getting. Social media is probably the most addictive element of our technology revolution, and for some people, going cold turkey and quitting may be the best answer. For others, creating new boundaries and using it more consciously is possible.

It's important for young people to understand the concept of object permanence—that they do still exist, vibrantly and meaningfully, even if they are offline. Digital expression should come second to real-life connection with peers, family, and community. If it's the other way around, it's a recipe for a lot of emotional hardship and misunderstanding.

SECURITY, PRIVACY, AND DATA SAFETY

In previous generations, when people went on vacation, they would make sure to create the impression they were still home: they'd make a point to set a timer for their lights; they would cancel the paper and have the post office hold their mail.

Today, people proudly announce on Facebook that they're on vacation somewhere fabulous. Recently, a client of mine did this. When he got back after his vacation, he had been robbed of tens of thousands of dollars of personal belongings.

Even when you choose to be very private about your personal information, security breaches can happen at companies that have your credit card or social security numbers. It used to be easy to maintain privacy and data safety, but with major hacks and leaks becoming common news, it's important take a second look at the ways we're sharing our personal information.

EXPLORING CREATIVITY

Much of the downside of the digital era is being a perpetual consumer of other people's ideas. While constantly being bombarded with marketing messages, we can get drawn into others' gravitational fields, slowly becoming passive "fans" rather than lead actors in our own dramas.

We are continuously encouraged toward voyeuristic tendencies by reality television shows that spy into others' lives, giving us access to information we really shouldn't know--or want to know, in some cases.

We may feel too insignificant to matter when there are those out there with 40,000 Instagram followers while we have only 129. We start feeling like life is a competition we're losing, which erodes the innate delight that comes from creative acts.

The antidote to that is exploring your own creativity. This can take many forms, but exploring new interests or revisiting familiar ones can increase our vitality and enjoyment of life. Affirming that you matter, whether you're validated online or in social media, is essential, and creating art can really help you to believe in yourself and practice gratitude for just being human.

There are countless ways to use technology to pursue creativity, whether it's shooting movies with your friends, taking an online cooking class, or learning to play guitar using an app. Very often, exploring new or hidden talents can be a catalyst for other positive changes.

GENERATION T

The "T" in Generation T stands for "tech." These are the digital natives, ages twenty and under, who don't understand the concept of buying a CD or looking something up in an encyclopedia. They have been born into unprecedented access to information and have a digital footprint from the moment their parents post a birth announcement. How are they being shaped in an era so profoundly different from that of their parents?

For many of these kids, seeing a picture of nature online is comparable to actually getting out there and experiencing it. They may have a hard time differentiating between the virtual and real worlds. Being physically out in nature—stretching one's limbs, smelling the green grass and the rain, interacting with a butterfly—all these experiences are lost today, unless they are purposefully pursued and encouraged.

Without a physical, visceral relationship with the natural world, we as humans can become very distressed and depressed. It's unnatural to spend ten hours on a phone rather than going outdoors and playing games with your friends, but this is the trend in younger people today, heading towards long, isolated hours online.

Just as adults need to set aside time to unplug and disconnect, so do kids and teens. In fact, the whole family should set aside time to play games and go on adventures without their phones. This might be met with groans and complaints at first, but it may also be the very thing that prevents your child from growing up depressed, lethargic, and disconnected.

BEING A DIGITAL ALIEN

My father just got his first iPhone. Every once in a while, I will receive a text message from him that's a colorful scribble. When I finally asked him why he was sending me those, he was dumbfounded. He didn't even know he'd been sending them.

Being a digital alien is nothing to be ashamed of—it's a generational quality, not something that reflects a person's intelligence. But in a world that's so drastically different from the one older people were raised in, a real sense of inadequacy seeps in.

Older people need to be included, not just to maintain their self-esteem, but for their survival. Many life-saving devices and apps rely on tech-savviness today. As younger folks, we can volunteer to help them understand the technological revolution in bits and pieces, and act compassionately as they make the leap we took so effortlessly. Seniors can also take classes in computers and electronics if they have the right attitude of openness towards learning, rather than resentment and frustration at being left out.

TECHNOLOGY AND HEALTHCARE

In addition to the technology revolutions that are facilitating medical breakthroughs, everyday people are the best equipped they have ever been to prevent serious illnesses. Fitbits are helping people keep track of how much they walk. People can plan healthy meals, find exercise plans, or take yoga classes on their phones. Unfettered access to information is allowing them to lead happier, healthier lives.

VIRTUAL REALITY

Virtual reality has many practical applications that are revolutionizing engineering, business and academic research. Today, surgeons use virtual reality to minimize risks during a complex procedure. They can practice removing a brain tumor, for instance, in a virtual space, and then proceed to the actual patient with exponentially more information and experience, preventing dangerous mishaps or errors. Today, pilots, astronauts, and military professionals train for high-stakes missions using virtual reality. They can simulate all kinds of potential scenarios and learn to minimize their risks in the field.

The brain can establish pathways and responses that translate into fewer accidents and more confidence performing challenging tasks. The potential for improvement in fields like the sciences and the military world through virtual reality is unprecedented; however, how will virtual reality in entertainment affect everyday people? Will virtual reality be the next addiction epidemic?

The fact that virtual reality can be far more entertaining and stimulating than real life means that it is a potentially massive marketplace. In the future, many jobs may take place in a virtual landscape as robots and AI begin to take over manual labor from the workforce. This may be a positive, in that it offers employment opportunities where none existed before, but it is also disheartening to imagine a whole culture springing up around an imaginary world. Of course, this has already begun to happen to some degree in games like Second Life, which has about 600,000 users today.

Virtual reality may represent a massively seductive exit from reality for people struggling with their appearance, their age, their income, or their background, since it's possible to be anyone you choose in a virtual environment. Time will have to be spent exploring the possible side effects of this technology and what safeguards need to be put in place to protect its users, both physically and emotionally.

TECHNOLOGY AND FREEDOM OF SPEECH

The average citizen has never had a voice like they do now. Even in repressive political regimes, citizens can utilize technology to organize and spread their message. The Arab Spring of 2011 is a perfect example of this. Longstanding undemocratic leadership in Egypt was toppled as a result of everyday citizens using Twitter to organize mass protests. Even in other countries that didn't experience the change of leadership that Egypt did, a message has been sent that citizens have more power than in the past.

North Korea is being infiltrated with smartphones against their leader's will, and little can be done to stop the impact this has had on the people, who are now able to see for themselves how the rest of the world lives. Nothing can stop the wave of technology as it sweeps the world, and not one corner of the Earth can hide from its reach.

These are the positive angles of improved freedom of speech. The negative aspect is that today it is easier for hate groups to find one another online, to assemble, and to recruit other members through online tactics. Similarly, groups that suffer from severe delusions or illegal sexual predilections such as pedophilia can organize, communicate, and grow. More complex laws will need to be developed to weed out the benefits from the drawbacks to an ever-increasing amount of free speech.

LANGUAGE

Language is constantly evolving, but it's been evolving at lighting speed in the digital era. A text message from someone in their twenties will differ drastically from someone in their forties. Different generations will use different spellings, sentence structures, and abbreviations. Capital letters are considered "shouting" to some.

Adding to our vocabulary, rather than replacing it, is key. It's always important to preserve the roots of our culture through literature and appreciate the great authors that have created so much beauty and richness for us to enjoy. When an entire generation can't spell and spends no time reading, we risk devaluing the English language to a dangerous point. Schools and parents need to help kids and teens to know the difference between standard English and the urban shorthand that is becoming so ubiquitous. Because when language dies, so, too, does original, critical thought.

Taking the Next Step

Learning to balance our online and offline selves is something every one of us in the 21st century is grappling with. Here are twenty affirmations I have created to help you achieve greater life/tech balance. You can print these out and hang them in your workspace, or you can record yourself reading them out loud and listen to them later. Any way that you use these affirmations is correct! Even if you merely read them one time through, they will help facilitate a healthier relationship with your phone, computer, iPad, tablet, and gadgets.

Affirmations for Technology

- I find it easy to achieve a balance in using technology.
- I choose to set limits on my technology usage.
- I limit my exposure to technology when needed.
- I turn off my phone and computer when connecting with others.
- I take time away from technology to connect with nature.
- My apps are in alignment with my goals and values.
- I release the need to respond to messages instantly.
- I practice self-discipline when using technology.
- I honor my body's limits and eat, rest, and exercise every day.
- I take breaks from technology often.
- I make the effort to represent myself honestly online.
- I cherish time spent in person with others.
- I respond to online threats appropriately.
- I take the time to protect myself through online security.
- I use my social media to uplift and inspire others.
- Today, I will allow my creativity to blossom, on or off the computer.
- Today, I will take the time to help someone younger than me to feel appreciated.
- Today, I will turn to offline activities when I feel lonely or bored.
- Technology is here to serve my purposes rather than the other way around.
- I find it easy and enjoyable to turn off my phone.

Chapter 12

BALANCE

"When I am in the heavenly light of my vibration, my
life is in balance & harmony."

—DEBBIE A. ANDERSON

Physical balance and coordination are things that we mostly
take for granted. Our ability to walk on two legs and ambulate
effortlessly around our environments, sitting, standing, lying down, all
without stumbling, is something we do without a second thought.

Within each of us is an innate, delicate, and complex mechanism that
helps us to navigate gravity and make necessary postural adjustments to
maintain our stability. Our vision, sense of touch, equilibrium, spatial
awareness, muscles, and hearing all work together to guide our actions
and keep us oriented.

Our bodies also have what is called homeostasis, the built-in ability
to control our body temperature, glucose, pH balance, and ions in our
blood. Our whole survival depends upon this internal system of detecting when things are in, or out, of balance within our bodies.

Life balance is similar, in that we have within us an innate sense of
how to achieve it. The more in tune we are with our inner "voice,"

whether through meditation, solitude, or conscious breathing, the more we are able to gracefully adjust to the challenges that life brings.

We all need to rest, eat, work, and play. We also need time for friends and family, and for our romantic partners; for personal fulfillment, spiritual growth, and the pursuit of our hobbies. We need time for exercise, sports, and adventure. We need vacation time. We need time to connect with nature and with animals, with the stars, the sea and the sun.

Within our relationships and within our work, we also need balance. At work, we need our efforts to be balanced by a return of income that is equal to our worth. We need to feel equality between our life outside of work and our time on the job. We need to receive as much love as we give, to experience a flow of reciprocal energy. And we need to balance time alone with our need for intimacy and connection.

Balance is an ever-evolving part of all our endeavors. It is what creates a sense of peace and emotional homeostasis. It's not a matter of spending X number of hours on any given activity; our balance for today will differ from what it is tomorrow, or next week. What works in terms of balance in your twenties will shift dramatically when you are in your fifties. There is no "perfect" way to achieve balance, because balance is about living with imperfection itself, shifting and adjusting rather than maintaining rigidity.

Just as your body will tell you when you're out of balance physically through feelings of vertigo or disorientation, so too will your mind and heart let you know when you're leaving out significant areas of your life that you need in order to feel whole. Learning to listen to those signals and understand them is integral to happiness.

A lack of balance may manifest as anger or as boredom, sadness, or despair. It may manifest physically, mentally, emotionally, or spiritually. Instead of trying to brush these symptoms under the rug, burying them under substances or compulsive behaviors, or simply denying them, we can heed their messages, turning inwards to examine exactly where, why, and how our imbalance is occurring.

THE ROOTS OF IMBALANCE

The thing about our sense of balance is that it tends to get established early in our lives. If we grow up in a home that provides us with adequate food, sleep, comfort, support, money, fun, encouragement, room to grow, education, etc., then we will simply continue on this path in adulthood, as habits tend to form and remain in place indefinitely.

However, if we grew up in a home filled with imbalances, then we may perpetuate these as adults without even realizing it. For instance, if we saw our father over-working, always running out the door to his job and never spending much time with his family, we may unconsciously memorize this behavior and repeat it as adults, not realizing that we are mirroring back actions that are essentially unhealthy and dysfunctional.

Similarly, if we grew up in a home where there was a strong emphasis on religion, prayer, ritual, and God, we may not have realized that there was a shortage of fun in our lives. As adults, we may end up being very serious yet sad, not understanding how important it is to balance our spiritual lives with the pursuit of pleasure, joy, and just kicking back.

In both examples, there is nothing inherently wrong with the behavior described—working hard or religious activities. In fact, both could be considered "self-care." The trouble comes when they take up the bulk of our time and crowd out the possibility of other types of self-care.

A lack of balance may also be masking trauma. If you experienced abuse of any kind as a kid, you may have inwardly steered away from intimacy and instead concentrated on accomplishments or a certain hobby. Later, as an adult, you may find that your personal life seems to lag behind your professional life.

In this case, fixing the lack of balance will not be as simple as just reorganizing your time. It will actually require facing deep wounds, ones that never healed, and working to take more risks to form healthy connections with other human beings.

THEORIES OF BALANCE

Many cultures, religions, and movements have their own understanding of balance, which we will explore below. Balance is such an important concept that these groups have created whole cultures and stories around the idea of living a harmonized, holistic life.

In fact, one of the most famous passages of the Bible concerns the concept of balance:

> "For everything there is a season, and a time for every matter under heaven: a time to be born, and a time to die; a time to plant, and a time to pluck up what is planted; a time to kill, and a time to heal; a time to break down, and a time to build up; a time to weep, and a time to laugh; a time to mourn, and a time to dance; a time to cast away stones, and a time to gather stones together; a time to embrace, and a time to refrain from embracing..." (Ecclesiastes 3:1-8)

Even in the creation story in Genesis chapter 2, we find that the Christian God did not subscribe to the idea of all work and no play. Instead, he decided to take a much-needed break after a week of hard work: "And on the seventh day God ended his work which he had made; and he rested on the seventh day from all his work which he had made." In Islam, we find the following passage about the middle ground in Ibn Manzur's classical Arabic dictionary:

> "Every praiseworthy characteristic has two blameworthy poles. Generosity is the middle between miserliness and extravagance. Courage is the middle between cowardice and recklessness."

THE AYURVEDIC THEORY OF BALANCE

Ayurveda is a healing tradition from India that literally means "wisdom of life." It is a science that not only helps to balance the body, but also the mind, heart, and spirit.

One of the main concepts in Ayurveda is the idea that each person is totally unique, with an individual mind-body constitution that requires its own approach. A person's health is measured not just in terms of their bodily functions, but also in terms of their emotions and the quality of their thoughts.

Imbalance (*vikruti*) is thought to underlie all illness and disease. Ayurvedic originators perceived that life existed on a dual plane of both spirit (*purusha*) and nature (*prakruti*), and that matter can never be fully separated from spirit. In other words, our health is holistic, and we must address all aspects of our lives to stay fit.

Ayurveda describes five states of matter, which are: solid, liquid, gaseous, radiant, and ethereal. Almost any material in the universe can be described as existing in one of these states. These states combine to create the three basic human constitutions (*doshas*): *Vata*, composed of space and air; *Pitta*, composed of fire and water; and *Kapha*, composed of water and earth. When all three of these are balanced, the body and mind are said to be in good health.

THE NATIVE AMERICAN MEDICINE WHEEL

In Native culture, there is such thing as a Medicine Wheel, which shows four directions, each representing multiple concepts. The idea is to move seamlessly from one quadrant to the next, balancing the four pillars of life—physical, emotional, mental, and spiritual. In the center of it all is self-love, self-care, and inner peace.

Starting on the right in the East, we discover the idea of the Spring and new beginnings. The color for this quadrant is bright yellow, reflecting the sunshine and the innocence of youth. The East represents creation and entering the world in our physical body.

Moving downwards to the South, the color has now changed to red, representing the hotness of the summertime. The lower quadrant is associated with experimenting, adolescence, and growth spurts. It concerns the emotions.

On the left is the West, projecting Autumn. It reflects wisdom and adulthood, celebrating the more mental aspects of life. The color is deep grey.

Finally, going upwards on the wheel we find the North, portrayed with the color white, an alloy of all colors together, signifying Winter. This is the quadrant of enlightened elders, who have been purified through the refining process of maturation. The spiritual life is now emphasized.

THE "MIDDLE WAY" IN BUDDHISM

As a young man, the Buddha was born a prince, experiencing all the luxuries, pleasures, comforts, and excesses known to man. He lived in a palace and was sheltered from all unpleasant people and events. However, he was deeply dissatisfied, sensing that there was a deeper reality to be encountered. He set out on a path to find a more enduring truth than the opulent life of royalty.

Out in the real world, the Buddha encountered sickness, old age, poverty, and death, which showed him the deep suffering mankind underwent. He then met a group of religious ascetics, who believed that self-deprivation in the form of fasting and inflicting bodily pain on oneself could end suffering and lead to a rewarding future in another life.

The Buddha at first sought the strict ascetic lifestyle of his spiritual peers. He gave up his family, left the city, and went to practice Sufism in a cave, all alone. He dove into a life of deprivation, renouncing food, sleep, and the company of others.

Near collapse, he was suddenly visited by a boy from the village who offered him a dish of sweet rice pudding. In a moment of grace, the Buddha made the decision to nourish himself. He saw the sweetness of the boy who desired nothing more than to help a stranger, and that kindness softened the Buddha's heart. He realized that he wasn't meant to experience life alone, but to accept help from others.

In a moment of full enlightenment, the Buddha realized that both self-indulgence and self-denial were extremes that kept him from being in the present moment, enjoying the wealth of beauty, wisdom, and peace that life offers. In that instant, he instinctually chose the "Middle Way."

As he ate the rice pudding, he found he missed his mother, his wife, his son, and all his friends. He made the decision to return home and live as a normal man. The ascetics judged him and rejected him, saying the Buddha had succumbed to hedonism, but that wasn't true. The Buddha remained committed to his inner search. But he knew his wisdom couldn't come from following the path someone else had dictated for him. He decided to seek his own truth within himself, living a balanced life of both inner spiritual work and outer service to others.

The Buddha compared the Middle Way to the strings on a lute. The strings couldn't be too taut, but they couldn't be too loose, either. There needed to be a balance of tautness and looseness that would result in the perfect conditions for music to waft through the air. He believed that balance itself was the recipe for the joyous eruption of harmony.

The Middle Way is about finding the balance between ambition and relaxation, between pleasure and discipline, between solitude and togetherness, between selflessness and self-care. It is about always being mindful of indulgence and deprivation, choosing to avoid extremes.

BALANCE WITHIN THE HINDU RELIGION

In Hinduism, followers are encouraged to seek balance between the four basic ambitions of life, which are called "*Purusharthas.*" These include *Kama*, the pursuit of pleasure and desire; *Artha*, the pursuit of material wealth and security; *Dharma*, the pursuit of duty to others; and *Moksha*, the pursuit of spiritual liberation and oneness with the divine.

Harmonizing the four life motives is one of the key goals in the Hindu religion. There is importance placed on wealth and pleasure as these experiences are part of being human; however, no one can live for wealth and pleasure alone, because to do so would deny the spiritual aspects of our nature.

When wealth and pleasure become the primary motives for existence, there is bound to be suffering, sickness and unhappiness. If self-gain isn't balanced with respect for others and the Earth, then the consequences are quite negative, as we see with the slow decline of our environment.

Taking the Next Step

On the next page you will find twenty affirmations for creating a more consciously balanced life, one which makes time for rest, relaxation, fun, dating, family, spirituality, exercise, sleep, work, and nature. But remember that you don't have to work with these around the clock. Easy does it; just read through them and feel their healing like a light, cooling breeze.

Affirmations for Balance

- I live a harmoniously balanced life that delights me.
- When I feel out of balance, I gently realign.
- I take time each day to enjoy myself and connect with others.
- I am at peace with myself and others.
- I release the need to compete with others.
- I get enough sleep every night.
- I make time for dating and personal relationships.
- I allow romance to grace my life and I embrace the magical.
- I switch between my many roles in life with ease.
- I set healthy boundaries on my time and money.
- I practice moderation and flexibility.
- I delegate tasks wherever possible.
- I balance the spiritual with the mundane.
- I practice gratitude for everyone and everything in my life.
- I honor my hobbies by taking time out to enjoy them.
- I balance my own needs with the needs of others.
- I surrender to the flow and stop trying to force things.
- I shrug it off when things don't go my way.
- I have a healthy relationship with uncertainty.
- I always balance work with play.

Chapter 13

LOVE

"The greatest thing you'll ever learn, is just to love and be loved in return."

—EDEN AHBEZ

Love is one of those words that gets thrown around so much that we've become anesthetized to its true meaning. It is used by many religions and spiritual communities, with or without its equivalent in action; it sees use in every pop song, in every soap opera, and in every greeting card; and it gets continually cheapened every time it's used to describe something more akin to lust, possession, trophy-hunting, hostage-taking, or co-dependency. Love may in fact be the most misrepresented word in our language.

But regardless of what we call it, we as human beings cannot live without love. Love is the life force from which we are born. It binds every living thing together, connecting us all in mysterious and beautiful ways. Love comes in a million forms: from romantic love, to love for one's country, love for one's family, love for oneself, love for one's art, love for one's city, and so on and so on, encompassing every aspect of that warmth inside our hearts we learn to nourish, share, and spread.

Love is greater than us and freer than us. It has no bounds and no limits. It cannot be bought or sold, cannot be traded or commoditized. You cannot make someone love you who doesn't, and you cannot stop someone from loving you who does. Love is beyond our control, and that is precisely why we fear it so much, crave it so much, and do crazy things to get it. Real love has no conditions, no agenda, no stipulations, no demands or ultimatums. It simply *is*.

WHEN LOVE IS MISSING

When we are cut off from love, whether through circumstances beyond our control, through trauma, or through withdrawing from life due to depression or anger, we suffer greatly. We are less productive, less happy, less fulfilled, and less confident. It is as though we are plants, and love is sunlight itself; when deprived of its brightness, we wither.

Understanding exactly why and how we cut ourselves off from the flow of love in our lives is a worthwhile, if challenging, process. There may be one specific moment when we felt deeply betrayed by others and made a mental pact with ourselves to never get hurt again; or, it may be a series of smaller, less definable moments in which we gradually lost our faith in humanity and allowed disappointment and disgust to close our hearts shut.

Childhood wounds such as abandonment, emotional, verbal, or sexual abuse, violence, and neglect can leave lifelong scars that make it difficult to trust love again. Very early on in our lives, we may have come to the false conclusion that "love doesn't exist," or "love only hurts," or "love is a joke." In fact, we may have come to these conclusions before we even had the language skills to say them out loud. Yet these patterns remain imprinted inside of us, damaging our relationships until we make the decision to heal.

We may be avoiding love in more subtle ways, such as by engaging in addictions that keep others at bay. Or we may be starving ourselves of self-love and focusing exclusively on love for and from others. There are a million ways to run from love, but thankfully, there are just as many ways back into love's arms.

THE CHARACTERISTICS OF LOVE

Love is made up of a variety of qualities that we all can agree upon, such as trust, selflessness, and respect. When one of these is lacking, we may question whether what we're experiencing can really be called "love." By exploring each individually, we can gain a deeper understanding of what real love entails and begin to rise to the occasion in our own lives.

Selflessness

Real love is about giving rather than taking. It means making sacrifices, small or large, to ensure someone else's safety, happiness, and security. What it *isn't* is being a martyr or giving from a deficit. Selflessness stems more from the idea of having a surplus inside us that overflows from within and choosing to give generously out of that surplus.

The odd thing is that this surplus comes from taking action to be less selfish in our lives. As we find that we have so much more to give than we expected, our delight in giving to others blossoms. Before we know it, we are filled to the brim with love.

We may have been hurt as children and determined it was best to look out for ourselves only, because no one else would. We may have decided a long time ago to be a lone wolf, looking out for number one, others be damned.

This is a very normal, practical response to abuse and neglect. However, it may have stopped working for us as adults, when we're called upon to be part of a community or to engage in relationships. Suddenly, our core coping strategy of selfishness becomes a liability and an obstacle to experiencing true intimacy with others. We need to learn to check our selfishness at the door and start finding opportunities to help and support our fellow human beings.

Respect

If you've ever walked through a forest, you may notice how there are trees of all heights. Short trees, baby trees, old trees, tall trees, and medium trees—yet all rise upwards towards the light, with each one having the same access to warmth.

In a lot of ways, respect is about acknowledging each person's right to the light. There is no one too small, too fat, too old, or too poor to deserve dignity, joy, abundance, and, yes, love. Respect means acknowledging differences while giving everyone to same access and opportunity.

Respect also means observing others' boundaries and listening to the messages they send, even non-verbally. To respect someone is to give them the space to operate autonomously and in their own best interest.

An example might be allowing an older person to take their time doing a task, rather than rushing them through it because we are bored or in a hurry. Another example might be respecting that someone's personal way of learning might be different than our own. They may learn visually through pictures rather than words, so instead of getting frustrated and trying to make them do it our way, we can practice respect for their limitations and preferences and offer solutions and alternatives.

Self-respect, on the other hand, comes from honoring our values and beliefs, from caring for our bodies and from keeping our word. Self-respect is a prerequisite for practicing respect for others because respect is inherently reflexive—we cannot give what we haven't got.

Trust

Trust is perhaps the most important and invaluable of the building blocks of love. Trust has many facets, including keeping your word, being consistently kind and reliable, and being able to keep a secret. Trust is established over time; it doesn't come overnight.

Many of us grew up in environments that were anything but trustworthy. We may have dealt with alcoholic or rage-aholic caregivers who we trusted not one bit. Or we may have experienced hot and cold emotions that left us confused and full of anxiety. We developed responses to these situations over time, so it's unreasonable to think we can heal our trust issues in a few days or weeks just by reading a few self-help books.

If we have dealt with a betrayal of our trust, we approach relationships more cautiously, being careful to vet the people in our lives before we commit to them or give them free rein of our hearts.

This cautiousness is *not* a bad thing. It means we are willing to trust again, albeit with conditions. We must learn to choose people that don't reopen our core wounds by acting unpredictably and erratically.

Trust involves giving another person the benefit of the doubt, even when proof of their affection is delayed in some way. If you send a text and don't get one back, you may become very upset and even angry. This is because you lack trust in the other person; believe that they care for you and will respond when they're available. Trust means having faith and giving other people the space they need, realizing it's not all about you.

Being vulnerable with others and telling the truth also requires a great deal of trust. We need to feel sure that we won't be laughed at, rejected, or abandoned. When we take the risk to be authentic, we build trust, giving our loved ones the chance to show their worthiness by embracing us for who we really are.

Trust begins within ourselves. Can you trust yourself? Or do you continuously fail to meet your own inner standards of behavior? Do you trust yourself to be peaceful, kind, and considerate? Or do you frequently lose your temper and lash out? Can you trust yourself to pay your bills on time, show up to work, and be present for those who depend upon you? Or do you often flake and make up excuses? Do not expect from others what we ourselves cannot provide. Trust is a two-way street.

Commitment

Love thrives on commitment. Commitment means making a decision and sticking to it, even when the circumstances become difficult. It means being there for loved ones through thick and thin, through poverty and wealth, through sickness and health, through youth and old age.

Commitment takes many forms—whether it's marriage, a committed partnership, a business venture, raising a child, having a dog, or pursuing an academic degree. Commitment provides us with self-esteem and enriches our faith in ourselves and in others.

Fear is the enemy of commitment. It tells us we're not good enough, that we'll never make it, that we don't have enough time, that we won't like something, that we'll change our minds. We get inside our own heads, staying aloof and withdrawn while never getting to experience the intimacy that commitment brings. We choose to remain in fantasy rather than daring to go through the unpredictability and uncertainty that are major components of commitment.

Our fear of commitment may have crept into our lives long ago. Perhaps our parents put too much responsibility on our shoulders and we revolted by becoming unreliable. Perhaps we merely copied the behavior patterns of uncommitted, inconsistent guardians. Whatever the reason, our lack of commitment in present day situations may be keeping us from really experiencing the love and inclusion we desperately crave.

Acceptance

When we love and accept others as they are, we don't constantly try to change them. We accept their flaws and imperfections, knowing that these come with being human. We don't idolize others or put them on pedestals; instead, we get to know and appreciate them for the authentic expression of their core essence, which is itself a gift from the Universe.

Acceptance means being open to differences in age, race, background, height, weight, attractiveness, intelligence, and income, acknowledging that everyone is worthy and comes with their own talents as well as their own struggles.

Just as with the other characteristics, acceptance of others is based on self-acceptance. If we are constantly berating ourselves, shaming ourselves, and rejecting ourselves, our relationships with other people will simply mirror these internal dynamics. We have to begin to inwardly accept our own limitations, knowing that we can then radiate this self-love outwards, into the world.

Part of acceptance is also shown in how we react when our affections aren't returned. Do we become bitter and resentful? Do we get angry at the other person or try to make them feel guilty? Do we threaten to kill ourselves if they don't immediately prove they love us?

Real love means accepting that other people might sometimes let us down, because they have their own feelings and their own destinies. We can't control if someone will care for us the way we care for them. All we can do is to give our love freely, without expectations or demands for reciprocity.

Forgiveness

Holding a grudge or harboring deep resentment for others keeps love from entering our hearts. Resentment and anger are natural, healthy reactions to abuse and mistreatment. If we were hurt, we may consider it "foolish" to forgive and forget.

Sadly, by holding onto these old hurts, we deprive ourselves of all the love we might experience in the present from new people.

Forgiveness doesn't mean that we are letting others off the hook for their awful behavior. It just means that we are choosing to let go of negative, limiting emotions that keep us trapped so that we can be free, happy, joyous, and productive. Forgiveness benefits us more than the people we forgive—that is its secret.

Most likely, the people that hurt us were themselves "hurt people." Abusers were usually abused themselves and are simply passing down what they know to be "normal." When people act out by cheating on, raging at, abandoning, or shaming another, they are really making a statement about themselves. It is never personal, even though we may spend our whole lives believing that it is. Forgiveness requires insight into others' fallibility, learning to see them as weak and crying out for help, rather than giving them the power to make or break us.

Again, if we want to practice forgiveness towards others, we have to first forgive ourselves. Have we been holding onto past failures, beating ourselves up for the things we've done wrong in life? Did we liquidate our savings, leave our partners, or drop out of school? Did we steal, lie, or cheat? Did we waste our time rather than spend it productively?

We must forgive everything if we really want to know and experience self-love. As adults, there are probably lots of mistakes we wish we hadn't made. But how we react to our missteps determines our entire attitude towards life. By forgiving ourselves, we open space in our hearts for love to come in and renew us. We *can* start with a clean slate, knowing that we are at peace with the past.

Empathy

Empathy is the ability to understand, relate to, and value the emotions of other people. To be able to put yourself in their shoes and walk a mile. To care for the welfare, safety, and happiness of others. Empathy is an inherent quality of love and is what allows for healthy relationships and bonds.

Sociopaths are people who are missing this vital quality of empathy. They see someone who is suffering and find nothing wrong in the situation, choosing to simply move on. They may have no problem inflicting pain because they cannot imagine receiving it.

Narcissists are another group of people who lack empathy. They can only see how situations affect them and their interests. For instance, when told that their employee's parent just died and the employee wishes to go home, they may become angry that production won't be met for that day and walk off in a huff.

Of course, not everyone who lacks empathy is a sociopath or a narcissist. Some people might simply get overwhelmed easily and find it difficult to comfort others. They may choose to withdraw or retreat when faced with someone else's pain and will often find it difficult to share their feelings in public. This type of person may care very much but choose to cry privately at home so as to never appear vulnerable.

Another type of person who seems to lack empathy may be the counselor or therapist who is simply burnt out on dealing with other people's problems. There is such thing as "compassion fatigue," which happens when you deal professionally with wounded people. People that work in emergency rooms, as field reporters for wars, or in the field of trauma in any way can get weary and find themselves not reacting properly anymore when their friends or family members express pain.

In a world where we are constantly bombarded with images of abuse, war, suffering, and poverty, we may become numb to the suffering of other people. We have to fight against this while also practicing self-care and keeping good boundaries. It's so easy to get sucked into the "news" and become addicted to tragedy. The news doesn't always tell us all the good things that human beings are doing for one another, or all the success stories of people overcoming difficult circumstances. We have to purposefully seek out good news to stay positive and uplifted in a world filled with sorrow.

Patience

They say that patience is a virtue, but it is one that can be cultivated through a conscious decision each day. Before getting into our car, we can affirm that we're not going to let traffic get to us, that we will be patient and perhaps even let someone into our lane without complaint. We can choose not to complain today that our partner isn't doing something we asked them to do a million times. We can let our kids be a little sloppy today without rushing in to clean up their mess.

Being patient means allowing others' feelings to develop at their own rate, rather than rushing them to feel the same way we do. It means waiting for a reply, rather than firing off a series of additional texts, emails, and calls because we need instant gratification. Perhaps it means letting someone makes their own mistakes and trusting that when the time is right, they will correct them without our intervention.

Patience means choosing goals that we may not be able to attain instantly, but which we rather have to work towards long-term, like pursuing a new career, starting a business, or building a stable relationship. These types of goals are often far more rewarding than short-term ones, but we must face the challenge of developing the quality of patience if we hope to succeed.

Peacefulness

Love is peaceful. It doesn't seek to create chaos, argument, or violence. It values calm—at home, at work, in the world, and in oneself. It may mean losing minor battles, letting minor infractions go, letting another person be right, or letting some else have their moment of anger without responding to it. Peacefulness is a daily choice to be a lover rather than a fighter.

Where does inner peace come from? And how can we cultivate it? The great spiritual teachers favor meditation as a way of going inwards, staying silent and tuning into the bounty of the Universe. Meditation can be an excellent way of quieting our minds of the endless chatter, of tapping into our inner wisdom and higher consciousness. The more we meditate, the greater our inner reserve is. When faced with difficult situations, we respond from a place of centeredness, intuitively knowing how to handle things.

If we grew up in an environment full of fighting, it may be the norm for us to meet insults with revenge or retaliation. We may equate gentleness and tranquility with weakness and feel that peace is the way of fools.

These attitudes are understandable responses to a childhood or young adulthood filled with violence. However, our reactions may no longer be serving our best interests. We may first have to grieve the loss of our youth. We may have to dig deep to connect with the fear that underlies our instinct to take revenge. But as we dig deeper, we will eventual come to see that peace is the only way out of the pain and despair. Taking revenge never achieves its intended effect of minimizing our pain. It only numbs us more and causes more regret and self-hatred.

Honesty

Love cannot abide dishonesty, because dishonesty is the enemy of intimacy. Being honest creates trust, comfort, security, and gratitude in our relationships. It is the foundation for all healthy bonding and communication.

If you are lying to others, you are depriving them of the chance to really know the authentic you. They may fall in love with you, but only for the wrong reasons, and will be sorely disappointed when the "real" you is revealed. Honesty is surely the best policy when it comes to showing your love.

Honesty isn't just about not telling lies. It's also about being emotionally honest with others, letting them know where we are at day by day. It's more honest to tell someone you're just getting to know them and feel warmly about the future, rather than to say you "love" them and not really mean it. It's more honest to tell someone you're afraid to commit than to falsely commit and then bail later.

Living an honest life extends to all areas. Are we financially honest? Do we cheat on our taxes or pad the expense account at work? If we're constantly looking over our shoulder about these types of things, we won't be available to receive the great love that is meant for us. We'll be too busy trying to combat the effects of our dishonesty.

Living honestly means that we do what we love and don't blame others for our unhappiness. When we live our truth, fearlessly pursuing our dreams rather than doing the work we think we're "supposed" to do, or that we think will make other people like us more, then we are more likely to attract others who resonate with our authentic frequency. Our honesty about our passions, opinions, and values will bring the right people into our lives while eliminating more superficial connections.

Honesty means telling the people in our lives that we love them—today. We cannot wait to give this message, because ultimately we don't know what the future holds. If you are lucky enough to have people you love around you, let them know—immediately. Don't hold back; share your feelings and trust that the Universe will reward your bravery one thousand-fold.

Taking the Next Step

The following twenty powerfully-crafted affirmations can be instrumental in helping you to receive the love you may be blocking out. Love is as integral to our well-being as sunlight and water. We cannot live without it. Say these out loud to yourself in the mirror, record them, email them to others, post them online. Get them in your blood and in your veins and know they are working for you even as we speak.

Affirmations for Love

- My heart is wide open and I welcome love into my life.
- I attract love and romance in magical and unexpected ways.
- I am magnetic and irresistible to my perfect partner.
- I am loved for being exactly who I am.
- My relationships are safe, fulfilling, and harmonious.
- Unconditional love is my birthright.
- I now allow myself to take "yes" for an answer.
- I am deeply worthy of love.
- I am constantly grateful for all the love in my life.
- The more I love myself, the more others love me.
- I am in total alignment with the vibration of love.
- I surrender to a supremely loving and benevolent Universe.
- It is safe to love deeply with intense passion.
- I am in love with every aspect of my life.
- I gravitate toward human warmth and affection.
- I attract only healthy, positive people into my life.
- Love is within me and all around me.
- I breathe in love and I breathe out forgiveness.
- I am whole and I am healed.
- Today I will have a loving intention towards everyone I meet.

Chapter 14

COGNITIVE DISTORTIONS

"The primary cause of unhappiness is never the situation, but your thoughts about it. Be aware of the thoughts you are thinking."

—ECKHART TOLLE

Cognitive distortion is a rather fancy, albeit clinical way of talking about the ways in which our minds play tricks on us. Cognitive refers to our mental process of judgment, memory, perception, and reasoning, and distortion means to be twisted out of shape, to be deformed or crooked. Thus, the literal translation for cognitive distortion is "crooked thinking."

Cognitive distortion is a concept coined by psychologist Aaron Beck, who developed Cognitive Behavioral Therapy (CBT) in response to seeing many of his clients suffering with negative beliefs about themselves that simply weren't true. He hypothesized that if patients could improve their thinking, they might improve their symptoms, rather than the other way around. (Beck's work was expanded and continued by his student David Burns in a 1989 publication titled *The Feeling Good Handbook*.)

Cognitive distortions tend to emphasize and perpetuate the bad thoughts we have about ourselves while convincing us these thoughts are coming from a rational, accurate place. Cognitive distortion often precedes, gives rise to, or worsens depression and anxiety. It can actually be harder to hear one's own voice giving criticism than if it comes from an outside party.

We may sometimes hear people mention "black-and-white thinking." This would be an example of a common cognitive distortion that keeps us from seeing the middle ground, or grey areas, in any given situation. There are many others that we will explore together in this chapter, such as overgeneralization, catastrophizing, using "should's," and filtering.

Unless we are actually suffering from a clinical psychological disorder, we *do* have a choice over our thoughts. And just as we might try to bring healthier foods, behaviors, and people into our lives, we can also exercise mindfulness around our thinking and speech.

But as you might imagine, it can be difficult to use your own brain to assess the health of your brain. It is often easier to work with a psychotherapist, who may offer more objectivity and can point out the cognitive distortions at work in keeping you unhappy or in a place of discomfort.

However, by becoming aware of the most "popular" or common cognitive distortions, you may begin to recognize them in your everyday life. This knowledge can help you to counter your own negative thoughts, by pointing out to yourself that there is no evidence to support the mean things your brain is telling you. The change in your thinking may happen slowly, but over time, you can begin to eliminate many of the most annoying cognitive distortions by simply refusing to buy into them when they arise.

THE ROOTS OF COGNITIVE DISTORTION

Many of us begin developing cognitive distortions very early in our lives as a defensive reaction to trauma. When adults are abusive towards us, it can be simply too overwhelming to accept the truth, especially if those adults happen to be our parents or caregivers.

Instead of accepting reality, we begin to create false presumptions that "explain" the adults' bad behavior. Many of these explanations center around "what we did wrong" that "caused" the adults to behave so poorly. In such scenarios, we may become hypervigilant, constantly scanning others' behaviors for signs of rejection or abandonment. We may develop the cognitive distortion of personalization or taking others' actions personally.

If our dad left the family and never came back, we may hypothesize that it was because we were not worthy enough. This personalization can extend into adulthood, when we may assume all kinds of independent events are our fault. Our boss may lose his temper, and we may assume this is because we are "bad."

This pervasive sense of responsibility for other people's misdeeds can cause widespread depression and despair, and all due to a distortion in our thinking refuses to place blame on the shoulders of the offenders.

There are those of us who grew up in an environment where rage and violence ruled supreme. Under such conditions, we may have falsely concluded that our own behavior could influence the rage-aholic's mood. If we were just quiet enough, good enough, sweet enough, perhaps they wouldn't yell so much.

As adults, this faulty thinking may have continued in the form of a focus on "should's." We may have constructed an inflexible world where we must do everything right in order to feel okay. With this self-righteous and controlling behavior, we alienate others and live under the tyranny of our own anxiety-producing cognitive distortion.

COMMON COGNITIVE DISTORTIONS

On the following pages, we will explore some of the most common types of cognitive distortions that take us out of reality. Some of us may suffer from just one of these, albeit in a severe fashion, or we may find that many of them seep into our consciousness on a daily basis. Remember that awareness is the first step towards overcoming your "stinkin' thinkin'."

Catastrophizing

Catastrophizing happens when we make a catastrophe out of an unpleasant situation—a mountain out of a molehill, so to speak. We may also practice catastrophizing by expecting a catastrophe in the future. Both of these thinking patterns arise because, in a strange way, it can actually make us feel safer.

Perhaps we were ignored as children and the only way to get attention was to have a catastrophe on our hands. Or we may have grown up in an environment where the more victimized we were, the more we were rewarded and validated.

Regardless of its origin, catastrophizing can cause a lot of unnecessary psychological distress. Instead of giving ourselves the benefit of the doubt, we rush to judgment before events even take place. We create a doomsday mentality which only perpetuates disappointment, hopelessness, and failure in an endless, self-fulfilling prophesy. We become paralyzed and full of self-pity, unable to see another alternative to the negative spin we have placed on our reality.

You can overcome catastrophizing by gently questioning the veracity of mental statements such as "I'll never," or "Nothing matter now," etc. Instead, you can say kind things to yourself, like "Everyone makes mistakes," or, "This is just a setback."

It will take patience and time to reverse a lifelong coping mechanism like catastrophizing, especially if it originated as a defense strategy in childhood. However, it's worth your time to heal your mind and it will get better with every step you take towards self-love.

Minimization

On the opposite end of the scale from catastrophizing is minimizing. This occurs when we underestimate the severity of a situation or downplay the consequences of our actions. We may do this out of denial, rationalizing what we cannot seem to take responsibility for; or we may minimize others' actions out of fear of conflict.

Some examples of minimization are calling a bullying incident a "joke," saying that an abusive partner is "just in a bad mood," or saying "it doesn't matter" when someone hurts our feelings. These are all examples of distorting reality, whether due to fear, guilt, shame, or a sense of futility over fighting back.

Minimization is a common cognitive distortion for those who grew up with alcoholic or dysfunctional parents. This type of child may have grown up cleaning up broken bottles, putting a blanket on a passed-out parent, or lying to teachers about a black eye. As an adult, this behavior may continue in other abusive relationships.

Others of us may have grown up in environments where we were rewarded for not calling attention to ourselves. The dysfunctional family may have preferred us to be invisible and in the shadows, so as adults, when we succeed or achieve, we minimize our accomplishments to perpetuate the family dynamic of secrecy.

It can be difficult to recover from minimizing, and sometimes it takes a third party to point out how serious our problems are. That third party may be a therapist, but sadly, it may also be a police officer or a doctor in the ER if our blind spot has caused us to break the law or become injured.

The first step is to begin taking our emotions seriously. If we feel angry, lonely, sad, or emotionally confused, we need to stop brushing it under the rug and really address our feelings as legitimate and appropriate.

Likewise, if someone's behavior makes us uncomfortable in any way, we have to accept this, instead of whitewashing it out of existence. Only then can we begin to set better boundaries and make better decisions about who and what we allow into our lives.

"Should" Thinking

Rigid, "should"-based thinking can create a sense of control in our lives, but it can also cause us to miss opportunities for joy, acceptance, and peacefulness. When we live in a tight little world of non-negotiable rules governing how other people should act and what should happen, we suffer tremendously when life goes off our script and into the unknown. It may fill us with terror when things don't go exactly according to plan.

We might get very angry at people over minor infractions such as being late or making a mess. Instead of asking others for what we need, we place unreasonable demands that drive them away.

Should thinking may be so pervasive that we don't even notice it's there. For instance, if we grew up in a family where every single person went to college and pursued a career in the sciences, our brain may tell us that we should take this same path, even if we would prefer to be an artist and travel the world. In fact, all our choices in life may be unconsciously molded by "should's," rather than by authenticity.

To heal from should thinking, we may have to spend time examining the origin of our rigidity and how at one point it may have helped us to survive a chaotic childhood. What was once a primary means of survival may now be a liability, keeping us from happiness. We can begin to soften our thinking, allowing for more flexibility, accepting others and ourselves exactly "as is." We *can* learn to feel safe in uncertainty.

Filtering

Also called tunnel vision or selective memory, filtering happens when we erase certain aspects of a situation and instead only focus on what we perceive as the negatives. We may focus so exclusively on the unpleasant details that we fail to see the larger picture altogether.

For example, it might be that we have one part of our job that we find very unpleasant. We may simply block out all the other things we like about our job, even the fact that we are employed while many others aren't in a difficult economy.

Mental filtering can be counteracted by a real effort to live in gratitude. This may mean making a gratitude list each day of twenty-five things that are working or going right about our lives. Even doing this for one day can change your entire perspective.

Consider how you are able to see, hear, eat, sleep, and function, all without any trouble. Or that you live in the United States, one of the most financially abundant countries in the world, where you are afforded a myriad of freedoms some groups would envy. In fact, the more time you take to really stop and evaluate just how lucky you are, the more likely you are to see a drastic change in your thinking.

Polarized Thinking

Black-and-white or "all or nothing" thinking eliminates the middle ground and instead pushes us into extremes. If we're not the best, we're "the worst." If we didn't succeed, then we're a failure. If we aren't the most attractive person on earth, then we are "ugly." And so forth. There is simply no grey area with this type of thinking pattern.

Polarized thinking is very childlike and often originates in childhood, where we learn to see things as either good or bad. Thinking in this way as adults keeps us from questioning our values. If we cast someone else as a monster and dehumanize them, then we don't have to explore our role or take responsibility for our part in any given situation. Conversely, polarized thinking may keep us from placing the blame squarely on the shoulders of those at fault if we mistakenly assume we are always in the wrong.

Healing from polarized thinking may require an admission that things are more complex than we realize. We may have to practice more forgiveness and more compassion towards others, seeing them as flawed humans.

It may mean practicing more humility, accepting that we don't always know the whole story behind what we see in any given moment. There are unseen pressures driving every single person, so acknowledging that we are not omniscient is a good step in the right direction.

Overgeneralization

Overgeneralization is often referred to as globalizing. It means that we take one or two incidents and use them to form our whole opinion of a situation or person. We take a single piece of evidence and make up a false story.

For instance, if we get rejected on a date, we may think to ourselves, "No one will ever love me." If a friend cancels on us one night, we may think, "So-and-so is lazy and unreliable." In this way, we seek to feel certainty in situations where we feel out of control.

Overgeneralization makes a certain kind of sense when you think about it. It's a defense mechanism that is meant to protect us from perceived harm. If something negative happens, we hope we can avoid it again in the future by making a "rule" about what it means.

But in the pursuit of safety from harm, we may actually be preventing ourselves from experiencing joy. Instead of understanding that rejection is part of any process, we see it as a sign we should give up. Instead of accepting that others make mistakes, we see their flaws as prompts to kick them out of our lives. In these ways, overgeneralization can end up isolating us and making our lives very small. Safe, but very small.

Personalization

Every little child believes that the world revolves around them and that they are the cause of others' behavior. This is a natural phase of development; however, once we are adults, we are intended to grow out of this as we realize that everyone has their own problems and issues and not everything is about us.

Those who suffer from personalization never grow out of that child-like way of thinking. They wrongly assume that every sideways glance, every angry gesture, and every unfair policy is a direct attack on them, one that is highly personal.

Taking things personally can give us a false sense of control. If we are to blame, then we can fix ourselves and thus remedy the situation. If we are not to blame, we may feel more overwhelmed with uncertainty, having to accept that the causes of events or others' actions may be totally unknown to us.

Healing from this type of thinking requires empathy. If someone shouts at us, we can think, "Wow, this person is very disturbed and seems unhappy." If someone cuts us off in traffic, we can think, "They would have done that to anyone because they are in a huge rush." We can gently give others the room to be imperfect and make mistakes, feeling confident in our own worth and value.

Control Fallacies

A control fallacy occurs when we assign another party an unreasonable amount of control over our lives. When we feel externally controlled, we may identify as a victim, believing that fate is against us. Additionally, we may have a fallacy of internal control, believing we have the ability to affect the outcome of events or dictate others' moods.

Both fallacies—of internal and external control—are false. We are never entirely helpless in any given situation, and we are never entirely in control. Even when we are seemingly helpless, we can still control our basic attitude towards events.

Fairness Fallacy

This occurs when our minds tell us either that "life is always fair," meaning if we see poor people suffering, we believe they must deserve it; or, when we habitually believe that life is "not fair," and continuously sabotage ourselves to maintain that false belief.

If we believe that life is meant to be fair, we may be grossly disappointed every time something doesn't go our way. We may feel entitled to a certain outcome, even when others don't agree.

Of course, fairness does matter. It *isn't* fair that men get paid more than women, and it isn't fair that people of color get disproportionately stopped by police officers while driving. However, it's how we handle these inequalities that matters. Do we become depressed, apathetic, and bitter? Or do we take actions to fight for justice and continue to affirm our worth and efficacy through estimable acts?

Each person has a different idea of what they consider fair, and learning to respect others' reality is an important step towards being healthy. We don't have to agree with everyone we meet, but we can at least try to understand them and empathize. Another way to think about this is that every villain is the hero of his or her own story.

Change Fallacy

In this scenario, we base our happiness on the idea of persons, places, or things changing. We find ourselves saying, "Life will be better when XYZ happens." The grass always seems greener in the future. Once we lose weight, we'll be happy. Once our partner stops smoking, we'll be happy. Once we get a new president, we'll stop being so depressed. Once we find a dating partner, we'll be fulfilled.

This type of thinking is so pervasive, there are whole industries that have sprung up to perpetuate it. Plastic surgery gives people the hope that they'll be happier when they look different, and the lottery gives people the hope that they'll be happier when they're rich.

The problem is that once we've achieved our goal, we tend to replace it with a new goal, keeping us on a hamster wheel of perpetual longing. Very rarely do we actually stop to appreciate what we have right now, where we're at, and the people in our lives at this very moment. By living in a state of striving for the future, we actually devalue the present moment, which is where all our joy lies. After all, the past is over, and the future is a mystery. The present, however, is a gift.

Emotional Reasoning

Emotional reasoning occurs when we mistake feelings for facts. Just because we feel a certain way doesn't make it true. Yet feelings can be so convincing, so total and unrelenting, that they make us question our entire reality. But as Nietzsche so eloquently stated, "There are no facts, only interpretations."

An example of this is the relationship between fear and danger. Just because you feel afraid doesn't mean a person or situation is inherently dangerous. You may be terrified to fly on an airplane, but that doesn't mean air travel is inherently unsafe.

Another example might be if, after a performance, you feel ashamed of how you performed. It doesn't necessarily mean you did poorly; there may, in fact, be no correlation between your feelings and the reality of any given event.

Learning to cope with feelings of anger, sadness, guilt, shame, loneliness, and helplessness is key in recovering from emotional reasoning. We have to give our feelings their due and allow them their space, while still reminding ourselves that there may be another reality outside the one we currently hold as gospel. A good step is to give ourselves twenty-four to forty-eight hours, when we feel overwhelmed, before making any major decisions.

Mindreading

Another type of cognitive distortion occurs when we believe we have the ability to read others' minds. We may not consciously see the absurdity of this, because it is an unconscious behavior we're hardly aware of. We fill in the blanks rather than live with the discomfort of uncertainty, and by doing so, feel safer in the world.

For instance, we may see someone we know with an unpleasant expression on their face and believe we know why. Or we may see someone make a poor life choice and believe we also know why they did it. The reality is, even with those who are very close to us, we always have to ask to make sure we know the truth. "Checking things out" by asking other people, "Hey, were you thinking this when you did XYZ?" is a great way to stay within reality rather than make assumptions. Other people will be grateful that we're giving them a chance to explain their reasoning. As the old saying goes, "When you assume, you make an 'ass' out of 'u' and 'me'!"

Always Being Right

You may have met folks who suffer from this delusion. No matter the situation, they always believe they are in the right. They will go to any length to assert their intellectual dominance. They will strive to win an argument, no matter the cost in terms of hurt feelings or broken relationships. In fact, they may end up alienating their loved ones, bosses, employees, friends, and family members, all due to a pathological need to be right.

Underneath this distortion may be a gross sense of inadequacy that the person will endlessly fight off. They may believe that, if they can just prove they are right, they will start to feel more worthwhile inside. This inner deficit drives all their actions, making them miserable, yet they continue the behavior.

For this individual, learning to live a more balanced, less perfectionistic life is essential. They will have to learn to derive self-esteem in a variety of healthy ways rather than through logical superiority.

Heaven's Reward Fallacy

This particular distortion occurs when we buy into the belief that all our hard work, self-discipline, and self-sacrifice will pay off in the end. Then, when the end comes and we don't get that big payoff, we may become depressed, apathetic, disappointed, and angry.

While hard work *does* tend to take us closer to a goal, it can be damaging to live in the future. It's always best to do work we love for its own sake, with or without a future reward. We have to strive to maintain balance in our lives, taking time to enjoy nature, friendship, entertainment, rest, and relaxation. In short, we have to create a heaven in the present moment, or risk feeling cheated when the end of the rainbow doesn't produce the pot of gold we had hoped for.

Taking the Next Step

Cognitive restructuring through affirmations is among the most powerful tools we have in creating a new reality for our lives. I've brought together twenty affirmations to help you reframe your problems, gather your resources and inner strength, and begin to recognize your own tremendous power and resilience.

Affirmations for Cognitive Distortions

- I embrace challenge as a way to grow.
- I have what it takes to handle whatever comes my way.
- I release the need to control people, places and things.
- I release the need to micromanage my life.
- Today, I will give others the benefit of the doubt.
- Today, I will question the truth of my own negative thoughts.
- Today, I will consider both sides of an argument.
- I accept and embrace the grey areas in my life.
- I now release the need to place "should's" on my shoulders.
- I release the need to minimize or ignore my feelings.
- Today, I choose to feel what I feel without running away.
- I release all self-hatred, guilt, and shame.
- I release all resentment, bitterness, and grudges.
- I offer myself and others forgiveness.
- I live in deep gratitude for my life.
- I gravitate towards loving, generous, and kind individuals.
- I surrender the need to know everything in advance.
- I thrive in uncertainty.
- I am open to possibilities I haven't considered.
- I accept that everything in the Universe is conspiring for my benefit.

Chapter 15

OUR STRENGTH

"Dig deep and empower yourself today. Stand in your inner strength. Be uniquely you."

—AMY LEIGH MERCREE

"Strength does not come from physical capacity. It comes from an indomitable will."

—MAHATMA GANDHI

We all know someone in our lives who exhibits extraordinary inner strength. We may call this person our "rock" and lean on them in times of trouble, or this person may be a role model of ours who we look up to and try to emulate. This person is able see calamities, setbacks, inequality, breakups, death, disease, and discomfort as lessons for personal growth rather than failures. They are able to thrive despite incredible odds stacked against them and come out the other side as a powerful and resilient warrior.

While we may admire this person and put them on a pedestal, perhaps even going so far as to call them a hero, the truth is that each and every one of us can cultivate our own strength any time we like by making a conscious decision to live in our most positive assets, affirming what is most noble in ourselves, and choosing to celebrate ourselves unconditionally for all that we have overcome, endured, and survived.

In essence, we can become our own heroes. And it starts the moment we start valuing our journey and having deep respect for our own process. Our strength comes from seeing ourselves in the divine light of perfection, knowing that we are perfect exactly as we are today, that nothing happens by accident, and that all of our struggles give us the insight and perseverance we need to move forward.

THE PARADOX OF STRENGTH

Strength is a paradox. It often relies upon vulnerability and flexibility, rather than might and muscle, as one might think. Consider the blade of grass that shoots through the concrete: its life force shatters dense matter, even though it is soft and delicate. By bending to the wind, it never breaks.

We may think it is stronger to hold all of our feelings in, to be "tough" and soldier through life. We may think it's stronger to be in control and dominate others. We may even think that it is an expression of strength to keep our pain to ourselves, numbing ourselves with substances.

But strength, as we said, is a paradox. The reality is quite the opposite of all these examples. The strongest position we can take is to surrender to our own humanity, acknowledging that we hurt, we feel pain, feel longing and despair, loneliness and disappointment. Allowing our tears to flow, our hearts to melt, and our faces to show our sorrow is the very definition of inner strength, because it shows the deep trust we have in life and in others to heal us.

To be a real leader, we have to listen, not command. We have to allow others to speak, to shine, to make their own choices. We demonstrate our strength through the love and respect we show, not by overpowering other people.

Strength is a paradox, because those that lead with an iron fist are eventually abandoned by those they govern. Conversely, those that cultivate kindness, acceptance, diversity, and empowerment remain beloved forever.

And what about the idea that numbing our pain with addiction will make us stronger? Every addict believes on some level that they are doing themselves a favor by numbing themselves so they can "deal" with life better.

But dependency is clearly weakness. If we are to face life, the strongest position we can take is to be free from substances, people, places, and behaviors that harm us. Addiction, once meant to help us cope, eventually drains us of all our power, emotionally, mentally, physically, spiritually, socially, and financially.

THE ROOTS OF COMPENSATION

We are at our physically weakest point when we are born. We are completely dependent on our caregivers for food, shelter, clothing, affection, support, love, and respect. Our utter vulnerability is either embraced and protected—or it is exploited.

If our caregivers shame us, abuse us, or hurt us, we will spend the rest of our lives trying to compensate for perceived weaknesses, developing a wide range of coping mechanisms meant to erase our "flaws."

If love is withheld in our family, we will believe that deep down we are unworthy and we will invent ways to compensate for this. These might include becoming emotionally withdrawn, becoming full of rage and driving others away before they can hurt us, or by becoming deceptive and deceitful to trick others into thinking better of us.

As crazy as it seems, a damaged person will go to almost any lengths in order not to feel the weakness, the powerlessness, of childhood. To heal, we may have to really sit there and re-experience what it means to be human, which is to be born undefended, naked, and alone, at the total mercy of others. In some ways, this total vulnerability is the human condition in a nutshell.

The weaker some people feel, the more aggressively they act. They may even resort to violence because they feel so deeply powerless inside to resolve their conflicts in any other way. A truly strong person will have the skill and resourcefulness to solve differences of opinion in a way that uplifts everyone involved, rather than trying to annihilate others.

What makes us strong is when we stop compensating, let go of the need to be better than we are, to be thinner, richer, younger, prettier, smarter, or even nicer. Inner strength means knowing we are enough, exactly as is, and refusing to doubt that perfect truth. Each one of us was born perfect and whole inside. There is nothing to compensate for; what we seek is already within us, just waiting for our recognition.

LIVING IN THE POWER OF NOW

There is so much we don't have control over in our lives. We are powerless over our families and how they treat us; we are powerless over the abuse or trauma we may have suffered in our lives; we are powerless over seeming acts of god, over death, and over disease.

But we do have the singular power to love ourselves in the present moment, taking action towards our own well-being. When we wake up each day, we can make the choice to honor, respect, and embrace our own journey. We can say positive affirmations instead of starting our day with criticism and self-hatred. We can choose to focus on our accomplishments, making a positive inventory of everything that we are doing right. We can refuse to let our assets slip through the cracks.

Rewiring the brain can start any moment you choose. Just because you beat yourself up yesterday doesn't mean today has to go the same way. In fact, you can even start saying nice things to yourself in the middle of the day!

If you have eaten poorly every day of your life, including today, there is still time to prepare a nutritious dinner for yourself. If dinner has passed, well then let me assure you, there is still a chance to make yourself a loving, nutrient-filled midnight snack!

Every moment is a *new* moment. Life is perpetually giving us second, third, fourth, and seventy-fifth chances to change. It's never too late to start being the person who you were always meant to be.

STRENGTHENING YOUR INNER COMPASS

Life will throw you curve balls, sneak attacks, and unexpected challenges—this is inevitable. But how well you respond depends on your own inner resources, not on external advantages. It will be more worth your time to go inward than to curry favor with the rich and powerful, get others to like you more, or read another self-help book from a self-help guru. The power that lies within you is your best chance at success in any arena.

So, just what actions can *you* take to strengthen this inner core?

SPEND TIME IN SILENT SOLITUDE

If you can't be alone, if you never go inwards and meet yourself in silence, you will never discover your best friend. You will be a stranger in your own skin. Solitude helps us to store up faith that we will be able to deal with anything that comes our way.

Solitude allows us to rejuvenate and heal from the slings and arrows of everyday conflict. In today's high-tech landscape, it also affords us the time to unplug from the phone, computer, laptop, email, and social media, remembering that we are human rather than machine. Solitude lets us hear our own thoughts, allowing us an opportunity to learn to trust and value them. It strengthens our intuition.

REVISIT WHAT HAS WORKED FOR YOU IN THE PAST

We've all had moments where our survival instincts kicked in and supplied us with a win. Moments where we surprised ourselves with inner reserves of wit, genius, or compassion that we didn't know we had.

Perhaps it was a moment where we rose to the occasion, standing up for someone more frightened than us. Or perhaps it was a moment when we took the risk to share our art with another person and they loved it. Maybe it was the moment when we took the initiative to protest something we felt was wrong and we were able to make a difference in our community.

Go back through your life and inventory these successes. Pinpoint those experiences where you felt you were most strong. What is the common thread? Who were you with? Where were you? How were you living? Looking to the past for clues about how to handle the future is always a good strategy. By doing this, you will achieve greater confidence in your resilience.

SEE THE BIG PICTURE

So often when we're in a crisis, we can't see the forest for the trees. We lose perspective and develop "tunnel vision." We lose track of who we used to be, because we're so focused on what's happening right now.

Step back for a moment and try to see the whole picture. See yourself as a child, an adolescent, and a young adult. See yourself as you will be ten years from now, or twenty years.

Connect to the pure, endless essence that is you. You will rise above your pain, and you will heal from your current circumstances. Life will start anew, and you will love again. Life is a wheel that keeps turning. Sometimes we're on top, and sometimes we're on the bottom, but we're always moving forwards.

LET GO OF ENTITLEMENT

While we all deserve success, joy, love and belonging, we don't automatically deserve a life without obstacles. If we believe life should be easy, we'll be gravely disappointed in the face of major setbacks. We'll take it personally, wallowing in self-pity instead of simply facing what is before us with the best tools we have.

Older generations had far more hardship than we do today. They had physical hardships, medical hardships, and a lack of technology and entertainment. They had far less access to the support of their peers, and less social freedoms and rights. Yet life went on, and all of us were born. They found a way to provide a future for us and a way to be happy in an imperfect world.

When we face a crisis, we have to let go of that sense of entitlement that says this shouldn't be happening to us. Instead, we can use our crisis to feel closer to others who have gone through the same thing. In fact, our crisis can be an affirmation that we are in solidarity with all other humans who feel pain, fear, sadness, and grief.

LEAN ON THOSE CLOSEST TO YOU

In times of struggle, it's always good to surround yourself with just a few trusted friends, family members or counselors who know the real you and have seen you through thick and thin. They will support, encourage, and love you through the darkest hours. You will be able to see your own strength through their eyes, even when your own eyes deceive you. These relationships are invaluable for this very reason. We sometimes need other people to reflect back to us our value when we are in a mire of self-doubt.

SURROUND YOURSELF WITH POSITIVE PEOPLE

On that same note, pay attention to the environments you frequent and the company you keep. Make sure you're surrounding yourself with people who motivate you, inspire you, and make you feel happy. Negativity and drama is contagious, so do your best to keep it out of your life.

KEEP A COMPLIMENT DIARY

Collecting and keeping tangible evidence of our worthiness is a great way to argue with your mind when it starts telling you you're a piece of crap. When someone says something nice to you, write it down in a journal. Do this every day. Every time a teacher, boss, friend, stranger, or dating partner makes a nice gesture or an effort to reward you, write it down. Collect emails, letters, gifts, and text messages that reflect others' love and respect for you.

When you're at your lowest point, go back and read these notes. Bask in their praise, knowing that you are appreciated. Use these keepsakes as contrary evidence to your self-doubt. See and feel the influence you have on others and how much joy you bring into the world. Let others give you hope, filling you with healthy validation.

IMPROVE YOUR PHYSICAL STRENGTH

Sometimes, if you're feeling weak inside, you can counteract this by placing a focus on building physical strength. The two are always going to be intertwined, so it's important that you not neglect your physical body if you want to feel really good about yourself.

You can lift weights, do pushups, or practice yoga, in which you use your natural body weight to build muscle. Take a hike through nature or run to build stamina. Find those activities that are just challenging enough that you can succeed at them but are not so easy that they bore you. Pick a physical goal and commit to achieving it. This can provide tremendous self-esteem, no matter how old you are.

DO THE THING YOU LOVE

Nothing will make you feel as strong as you do when you're doing something you enjoy. When you're in your element, whether it's telling jokes, writing stories, making music, taking care of animals, fixing old cars, or skateboarding, you will feel powerful. And your power will come not from external awards or recognition, but from the sheer joy you feel just being yourself.

Make time for this treasured activity in your life. Clear your schedule at least one day a week to get your endorphins flowing again by being in your own personal "happy place." Don't let anything else interrupt you or get in your way.

HELP OTHERS

As strange as it may sound, helping other people gives us the feeling of strength in our lives. It is an empowering action that reminds us that we always have something to give, and we can always make a difference.

We may have very little political power in our own eyes, but we can use our voice to speak up for those less fortunate. We can donate our time or provide others with mentorship. We can lend a hand to organized events or create our own events that benefit other people.

Giving back multiplies the flow of positive energy in our lives. We see ourselves in the new light of generosity of spirit, and this estimable action translates into higher self-esteem in general. We know that we are connected, and we start to feel a sense of community with every person we meet.

PERSONAL EMPOWERMENT CHECK-LIST

And finally, an empowerment checklist to help you successfully identify the areas in your life where you're weakening yourself, and those areas you can focus on to build up your strength—physically, mentally, emotionally, and spiritually:

Exactly how and when do we give away our power?

We give away our power when…

- We compare ourselves to other people instead of acknowledging that each person has a unique journey and can only be compared to themselves.

- We rush and care only about the result and not about the journey.

- We let negative, judgmental thoughts cloud out our understanding of our own gifts, talents and abilities.

- We let others define us, rather than defining ourselves.

- We lie, act disingenuously, or people please.

- We compulsively place others' needs above our own.

- We also give away our power—the power to do good—when we focus exclusively on ourselves and ignore others' needs.

- We ignore our thoughts, feelings, and opinions, refusing to listen to our inner voice.

- We don't take good care of our bodies.

- We buy into quick fixes instead of getting to the root of our issues.

- We betray our deepest values and settle for an inauthentic existence.

What does it mean to be empowered?

We are empowered when…

- We slow down and ground ourselves in the present moment.

- We ask others for their support and acknowledge we can't do it all alone.

- We honor our feelings and listen to them.

- We speak our truth in a respectful, peaceful, kind way.

- We own our gifts and refuse to hide them.

- We speak well of ourselves and affirm our highest good out loud.

- We forgive easily and speak well of others.

- We are empowered by the healthy, supportive people we surround ourselves with.

- We nourish our bodies, feed our minds, and sleep well.

- We have a purpose and direction in our lives.

- We help others.

- We act creatively, reflecting on our divine penchant for creativity.

Taking the Next Step

I leave you with a series of affirmations that you can take with you wherever you go to maximize your personal inner strength.

You can say these to yourself in the mirror, record yourself saying them out loud to listen to in the car, or put them on post-it notes around the house. Consistency is more important than volume.

Pick one to say to yourself each day and allow it to change you. Feel it seep into your neurons, knowing that your brain is rewiring for your greatest good RIGHT NOW!

I believe in you. You are worthy of new thought habits, mental, emotional, physical, and spiritual health, change, love, fulfillment, meaning, and a rewired life!

Affirmations for Rewiring Your Life

- I can handle anything that comes my way.
- I am strong, brave, creative, and resourceful.
- I am connected to the limitless power of the Universe.
- I am connected to everyone and everything. .
- I have what it takes to face life on life's terms.
- I am confident and radiant confidence to the world.
- I am bold. I take chances and healthy risks every day.
- Every day I get stronger—physically, mentally, emotionally, and spiritually.
- I am strong, beautiful, and powerful beyond measure.
- I have the ability to change my life.
- Today I will acknowledge my talents, my intelligence, my beauty, and my resilience.
- Today, I will honor my feelings and listen to them.
- The past has no power over me anymore.
- I make the right decisions for myself and let go of my self-doubt.
- I interpret my setbacks as stepping-stones to success.
- I respond to challenges with enthusiasm and grace.
- I welcome all opportunities for growth and empowerment that life provides.
- I take control of my destiny.
- I have unshakable faith in myself today.
- I live in deep alignment with my core values.
- I live in deep alignment with my most authentic desires.
- I always do my best.

- I always reward my best efforts.
- I am unstoppable.
- I am internally guided by my soul's highest good.
- Each day I surprise myself with my own inner strength and fortitude.
- I am filled with positive energy and lust for life.
- I am filled with gratitude for all that life has given to me.
- I am connected to the divine intelligence that is pure love.
- I open my heart to infinite possibility.
- There are always solutions that I haven't thought of yet.
- I now forgive myself for every single thing that happened in the past.
- I am now free of the influence of the past.
- Each day, I am healing deeply.
- I am proud of my unique contribution to the world.
- I am patient with myself and others, always.
- I am kind to myself and others, always.
- I stand up for myself and others, always.
- I am balanced and strong no matter who I am with.
- I hold my head up high and straighten my back.
- I take full responsibility for my own happiness.
- I am willing to create new healthy habits.
- I am divinely worthy.
- I am constantly improving.
- I breathe into the deepest expression of my most authentic self.

ACKNOWLEDGMENTS

would like to express my utmost appreciation to all my loved ones, teachers, clients, mentors, friends, and colleagues who have shared their experiences with me. It is you who inspired me to write this book, and it is your stories that have influenced these pages.

To my husband, Marcin: I am forever grateful that I get to spend my life with you and for finding you. Thank you for believing in me and showing me endless love, encouragement, strength, and stability. You are my greatest gift.

To my mother: your unconditional love allowed me to always feel safe and know that everything would be okay in life. Your knowledge and spirit has helped to shape who I am today and pushed me to always persevere.

To my father: I am thankful for you. You always pushed me to be my best self and you tell me how proud you are all the time. I know that I can do anything in this life because of your encouragement.

To my brothers, Max, Jordan, and Joe: you are three shining examples of good-hearted, kind, sincere and emotionally aware men who make this world a better place.

To my stepmom, Jayne: thank you for your consistent support, love, and strength through the many chapters of my life.

To my in-laws, Grazyna and Izydor: yes, by law you are now another mother and father in my life, and I am so lucky to have your love, energy, encouragement, and constant faith in me.

To my dearest friends, who have always been there for me: I love you all deeply.

To my beautiful family, Jessica, Jean, David, Sandy, Elyse, Aaron, Alex, Olivia, Papa, Fred, Bari, and Carrie: I love you and am so grateful for your unconditional love.

To Linda Romano, my right- and left-hand woman, who has helped me build *Rewired* from the beginning and who is the producer of my podcast, Rewired Radio: your support, commitment, consistency, and presence is such a blessing in my life.

To my publishers, Andrew Flach and Ryan Tumambing, along with editor Ryan Kennedy: thank you so much for your assistance, faith, hope, and your help in bringing this book to life.

Lastly, to my little one that is yet to emerge into this outside world: this book is for you. I hope this comprehensive guide helps you and all of us to see our own light, know peace, seek balance, and just simply live in love.

ABOUT THE AUTHOR

Erica Spiegelman is an author, addiction and wellness specialist, and motivational speaker who works with individuals, couples, and families on personal growth and overall wellness. Erica provides a holistic approach to helping people overcome their struggles with addictions and dependency and gives them the tools they need to create healthy lives for themselves.

Erica is the author of *Rewired: A Bold New Approach to Addiction & Recovery,* the *Rewired Workbook,* and the *Rewired Coloring Book.*

Erica holds a bachelor's degree in literature from the University of Arizona and is a California State Certified Drug and Alcohol Counselor (CADAC)-II from UCLA. A regular contributor to online health outlets, TV news shows, and host of "Rewired Radio" on RadioMD, Erica also writes for Maria Shriver.

Through her work, writing, and media appearances, Erica is dedicated to touching and changing as many lives as possible.